Practical English Language Teaching: Young Learners

By Caroline T. Linse

Series Editor: David Nunan

Practical English Language Teaching: Young Learners

Published by McGraw-Hill ESL/ELT, a business unit of the McGraw-Hill Companies, Inc., 1221 Avenue of the Americas, New York, NY 10020. Copyright © 2005 by the McGraw-Hill Companies, Inc. All rights reserved. No part of this publication may be reproduced or distributed in any form or by any means, or stored in a database or retrieval system, without the prior consent of The McGraw-Hill Companies, Inc., including, but not limited to, in any network or other electronic storage or transmission, or broadcast for distance learning.

ISBN: 0-07-310308-X
1 2 3 4 5 6 7 8 9 DOC/DOC 11 10 09 08 07 06 05

ISBN: 0-07-111841-1 (International Student Book)
1 2 3 4 5 6 7 8 9 DOC/DOC 11 10 09 08 07 06 05

Editorial director: Tina B. Carver
Executive editor: Erik Gundersen
Development editor: Linda O'Roke
Production manager: MaryRose Malley
Cover designer: Martini Graphic Services, Inc.
Interior designer: Acento Visual
Photo researcher: David Averbach

INTERNATIONAL EDITION ISBN: 0-07-111841-1
Copyright © 2005. Exclusive rights by The McGraw-Hill Companies, Inc., for manufacture and export. This book cannot be re-exported from the country to which it is sold by McGraw-Hill. The International Edition is not available in North America.

The *McGraw-Hill* Companies

In Memory of Kathryn Z. Weed
who helped teachers the world over respect
and honor their young learners' cultural heritages

Acknowledgements

The author and publisher would like to thank the following individuals who reviewed the *Practical English Language Teaching* books manuscripts at various stages of development and whose commentary was instrumental in helping us shape these professional reference volumes:

Kathleen M. Bailey, Monterey Institute of International Studies, Monterey, California, USA

Ronald Carter, Centre for English Language Education, Department of English Studies, University of Nottingham, UK

Andy Curtis, The English School, Kingston, Ontario, Canada

Nicholas Dimmitt, Asian Institute of Technology, Pathumthani, Thailand

Fernando Fleurquin, University of Ann Arbor, Michigan, USA

Donald Freeman, School for International Training, Brattleboro, Vermont, USA

Donald Occhuizzo, World Learning/School for Internacional Training; formerly Alumni, Sao Paulo, Brazil

Betsy Parrish, Hamline University, St. Paul, Minnesota, USA

Michael Rost, Author/Researcher, San Francisco, California, USA

Kathy Z. Weed

In addition, I'd like to thank the following people:

David Nunan, the McGraw-Hill editorial team, and Kathy Weed, my critical buddy, who provided invaluable perspectives regarding the education of children developing English language skills. Also, thank you to Lisa Cummins, Jean Lowe, Fran Gamoba, Carolina Rivera, Linda Quintanilla, the faculty and students at Sookmyung Women's University in Seoul, Korea and the Dept. of Lexicology at Minsk State Linguistic University in Belarus for their helpful insight. Finally, thanks to Joel McKee and Josh Berkowitz for allowing the use of their artwork.

This book is dedicated to my mother–Barbara Susan Bucher Linse, who taught me the value of words, teaching, and love.

Table of Contents

Acknowledgements . . . . **iv**

Foreword . . . . **vii**

Chapter **One**

The child as a language learner **1**

1. Introduction **2**
2. What is developmentally appropriate instruction? **2**
3. Learning about children's development and interests **6**
4. Children's language learning and acquisition **12**
5. Making input meaningful to learners **13**
6. Supporting children's language acquisition and learning **14**
7. Conclusion **16**
Further readings **17**
Helpful Web sites **17**
References **18**

Chapter **Two**

Teaching listening to young learners **21**

1. Introduction **22**
2. What is listening? **22**
3. Background to the teaching of listening **25**
4. The development of listening skills **27**
5. Classroom techniques and activities **29**
6. Listening in the classroom **40**
7. Conclusion **43**
Further readings **43**
Helpful Web site **43**
References **44**

Chapter **Three**

Teaching speaking to young learners **45**

1. Introduction **46**
2. What is speaking? **46**
3. Background to the teaching of speaking **47**
4. The development of speaking skills **49**
5. Classroom techniques and activities **52**
6. Managing speaking activities **62**
7. Speaking in the classroom **63**
8. Conclusion **66**
Further readings **66**
Helpful Web sites **66**
References **67**

Chapter **Four**

Teaching reading to young learners **68**

1. Introduction **69**
2. What is reading? **69**
3. Background to the teaching of reading **71**
4. The development of reading skills **75**
5. Classroom techniques and activities **78**
6. Reading in the classroom **90**
7. Conclusion **94**
Further readings **94**
Helpful Web sites **94**
References **95**

Chapter **Five**

Teaching writing to young learners **97**

1. Introduction **98**
2. What is writing? **98**
3. Background to the
   teaching of writing. **99**
4. Development of writing skills . . . **101**
5. Classroom techniques
   and activities **110**
6. Writing in the classroom **114**
7. Conclusion **117**
Further readings **118**
Helpful Web sites **118**
References **119**

Chapter **Six**

Teaching vocabulary to young learners **120**

1. Introduction **121**
2. What is vocabulary? **121**
3. Background to the
   teaching of vocabulary **122**
4. Principles for teaching
   vocabulary **123**
5. Classroom techniques
   and activities **128**
6. Vocabulary in the classroom **132**
7. Conclusion **134**
Further readings **135**
Helpful Web sites **135**
References **135**

Chapter **Seven**

Assessing young learners **137**

1. Introduction **138**
2. What is assessment? **138**
3. Background to assessing
   young learners **141**
4. Formal assessment **143**
5. Classroom-based assessment **145**
6. Assessment in the classroom **157**
7. Conclusion **162**

Further readings **162**
Helpful Web sites **163**
References **163**

Chapter **Eight**

Working with parents of young learners **165**

1. Introduction **166**
2. Why are parents important? **166**
3. Ways that parents can be
   involved and connected **167**
4. Creating a teacher-parent
   partnership **170**
5. Conclusion **184**
Further readings **184**
Helpful Web sites **184**
References **185**

Chapter **Nine**

Key issues in teaching young learners **186**

1. Introduction **187**
2. Classroom management **187**
3. Special needs **192**
4. Multiple intelligences **197**
5. Tutoring **198**
6. Technology **199**
7. Professional support **200**
8. Conclusion **201**
Further readings **201**
Helpful Web sites **201**
References **203**

Appendix Children's songs
and finger-plays **204**

Glossary **207**

Index **211**

Credits **216**

Foreword

Vision and purpose

The *Practical English Language Teaching* series is designed for practicing teachers or for teachers in preparation who may or may not have formal training in second and foreign language teaching methodology. The core volume in this series, *Practical English Language Teaching,* provides an overall introduction to key aspects of language teaching methodology in an accessible yet not trivial way. The purpose of this volume is to explore issues as they relate directly to the teaching of English to young learners. The focus of this volume is on the education of children who are between the ages of five and 12 years of age.

This volume draws upon and combines content from three different professional arenas. First, this book is based on developmentally appropriate practices because it is necessary to always consider the children's physical, emotional, and cognitive development. Second, this volume considers both the abilities of native English speakers and the English content they are taught because children learning English as a Second or Foreign Language should not be expected to do something in English that would be beyond the reach of a native speaker. In addition, there are many strategies and techniques which are effective for children learning English as a native language that can be adapted to the ESL and EFL classroom. Finally, this book draws upon applicable content related specifically to ESL and EFL. Information, strategies, and techniques used with learners over 12 have been carefully selected and adapted for use with young learners.

Features

- A clear orientation and introduction to the teaching of English to young learners including a brief overview of young learner development. Information is provided for teachers working in both Foreign Language and Second Language contexts.

- Reflection questions inviting readers to think about critical issues in young learner language teaching and Action activities requiring readers to apply the ideas, principles, and techniques to the teaching of young learners in their own situations.

- A detailed treatment of teaching English to learners who may or may not possess literacy skills in their native language.

- Numerous practical illustrations from a wide range of coursebooks and extracts from authentic classroom interactions.

- Information on how to effectively work with the parents of young learners even when the parents do not speak English.

- A key issues chapter which provides suggestions for dealing with classroom management, special educational needs, technology, tutoring, and professional organizations.

- Charts and checklists of useful information for the young learner teacher.

- Reproducible material for direct application of content to in-class lessons.

- Suggestions for books, articles, and Web sites offering resources for additional up-to-date information.

- An expansive glossary offering short and straightforward definitions of language, early childhood, and education teaching terms.

Audience

As with the core volume, this book is intended for both experienced and novice teachers. It should be of interest to teachers who have experience teaching as well as those who are preparing to join the profession. It is of interest to parents of young learners who want to be in a better position to help their children learn English. It is also intended for teachers who may have had experience working with learners over the age of 12, but who are new to the world of young learners. This volume is also useful for individuals who may not have experience teaching young learners but have responsibilities for supervising teachers of young learners or designing English as a Foreign Language and English as a Second Language programs for young learners.

Overview

Chapter 1

This chapter provides a brief overview of child development as well as ways to learn about children's development and interests. The differences between language acquisition and language learning are discussed in addition to ways to support children's learning.

Chapters 2–5

In this volume, like the core volume, each skill area–listening, speaking, reading, and writing–has its own chapter. Although an approach that integrates all different skill areas is advantageous, in order to better understand the role of individual skill areas each one received its own separate chapter.

Chapter 6

This chapter includes the latest vocabulary development research as it applies to young learners.

Chapter 7

This chapter explains the importance of working with parents as well as strategies which can be used to create a positive home-school connection.

Chapter 8

This chapter provides information on how to assess both oral and written language skills in a young learner program.

Chapter 9

This chapter deals with key issues facing teachers of young learners.

Chapter **One**

The child as a language learner

Goals

At the end of this chapter, you should be able to:

 describe developmentally appropriate instruction.

 identify examples of cognitive, emotional, physical, and moral development in children.

 explain ways to learn about children's development and interests.

 distinguish between language acquisition and language learning as it relates to children.

describe techniques for finding out about the needs and interests of young learners.

1. Introduction

The aim of this chapter is to provide an overview of some of the issues related to children's overall development as well as their language development. We will begin with information about developmentally appropriate instruction and three major areas of children's development: social-emotional, cognitive, and physical. We will then move to suggestions for learning about children's development and interests. Then the distinction between language acquisition and language learning is provided. Finally, ways to make input comprehensible and to support children's language development are discussed.

2. What is developmentally appropriate instruction?

Experienced early childhood professionals encourage **caregivers** and teachers of young learners to provide **developmentally appropriate instruction.** (For the purposes of this book, young learners are defined as children between the ages of 5-12.) By the very nature of your job as a teacher of young learners, you must be aware of children's basic physical and psychological needs. Teachers of young learners should provide the care necessary to meet these needs so that they can thrive and focus on learning. In other words, teachers of young learners have two jobs: to provide care and to provide instruction. In order to provide the best possible instruction, you need to adjust educational experiences to meet the developmental stages of the individual child. It is important to give children challenges that they are developmentally ready to meet.

It is never too late to learn, but sometimes it is too early.

For example, a child who cannot recognize the numbers between 1 and 100 is not ready to do multiplication. A child who has developed strong oral-language skills in her native language is better prepared to begin reading than a child who has not. A young learner who can comprehend a sequence of events is better prepared to understand a story than a child who cannot.

Developmentally appropriate practices

In addition to educators, doctors specializing in child development also encourage caregivers to adjust to a child's individual stages and rates of development. Children require and deserve professionals who interact with them in appropriate ways based on the child's **social/emotional, physical, cognitive,** and **moral development** (Brazelton and Greenspan, 2000). Children develop emotionally, morally, physically, and cognitively at different rates. One child may not be bothered when he is accidentally pushed by another child, while a different child may burst into tears when children look at him in a mildly negative manner. Some children will understand the necessity to share food and toys, while others will believe that if it is theirs, they should keep it. One child may be able to hop at a very early age, while another may struggle for years with the skill. There are children who will quickly grasp sound-symbol relationships, whereas it will take others a longer period of time to comprehend this concept.

By being aware of what children can and can't do developmentally, teachers are better able to provide appropriate learning experiences for their young learners. As a teacher, I try to look beyond a child's age and observe her development to determine what she can and can't do. This makes it possible for me to give my young learners tasks which are within their reach, tasks where they will succeed and experience success. This success gives them the confidence to attempt tasks which are progressively more difficult.

Attributes of development

Figures 1, 2, and 3 on pages 4 and 5 highlight attributes of development in three areas: social/emotional, cognitive, and physical development. The attributes are observable and can help you become more aware of different aspects of individual children's development. Figures 1-3 are guides to help you develop a greater sense of your young learners' individual development. If you are aware of your students' strengths as well as areas where they may need a little extra help or assistance, it will be easier for you to plan appropriate instruction.

Attributes of Emotional/Social Development

Is usually in a positive mood

Is not excessively dependent on adults

Usually copes with rebuffs adequately

Has positive relationships with one or two peers; shows the capacity to really care about them and miss them if they are absent

Displays the capacity for humor

Does not seem to be acutely lonely

Approaches others positively

Expresses wishes and preferences clearly; gives reasons for actions and positions

Asserts own rights and needs appropriately

Is not easily intimidated by bullies

Expresses frustrations and anger effectively and without escalating disagreements or harming others

Gains access to ongoing groups at play and work

Enters ongoing discussion; makes relevant contributions to ongoing activities

Takes turns fairly easily

Shows interest in others; exchanges information with and requests information from others appropriately

Negotiates and compromises with others appropriately

Does not draw inappropriate attention to self

Accepts and enjoys peers and adults of ethnic groups other than his or her own

Figure 1 Attributes of Emotional/Social Development

Attributes of Cognitive Development

Can follow one-step instructions

Can follow two-step instructions

Can follow three-step instructions

Understands the concept of symbols such as numbers and letters

Is interested in academic content

Likes reading or being read to

Likes playing with words, numbers, or abstract symbols

Figure 2

Grasps concrete and/or abstract concepts easily

Can make connections between different concrete concepts

Can make connections between abstract and concrete concepts

Can make connections between different abstract concepts

Comprehends concrete and/or abstract cause and effect relationships

Can recognize patterns

Can follow a sequence of events

Can classify concrete pictures, objects, and/or abstract concepts

Figure 2 Adapted from Attributes of Cognitive Development

**Attributes of Physical Development –
Fine Motor and Gross Motor Skills**

Demonstrates muscle control when using scissors

Demonstrates muscle control when using fat crayons, pencils, or markers

Demonstrates muscle control when holding chop-sticks, spoons, forks, or knives

Demonstrates muscle control when using skinny pencils, markers, or crayons

Demonstrates muscle control when using paintbrushes

Demonstrates the muscle coordination necessary to throw or kick a ball

Demonstrates the muscle and hand-eye coordination necessary to catch a ball

Demonstrates muscle control and foot-eye coordination necessary to kick a ball when rolled

Demonstrates hand-eye coordination necessary to hit a ball when thrown as in tennis, baseball, or volleyball

Is able to skip, hop, run, jump, and dance or move to music

Figure 3 Attributes of Physical Development
(Figures 1–3 adapted from McClellan and Katz, 2001)

Inconsistent development

A specific child does not develop in all areas at the same rate. Children who are considered to be intellectually gifted are also often considered to be emotionally young. A child may learn to read at a very early age and have developed advanced cognitive skills but behave in ways that are viewed as emotionally and socially immature.

Think of a child you know. The child may be a student you have now or someone in your family. Describe one or more of the children you listed. Be sure to give examples of their physical, cognitive, and social/emotional development.

Example:

Child: Anwar is five years old.
Social/Emotional Development: He uses words and not tears or fists to tell others that he is upset.
Cognitive Development: He can follow two-step instructions such as put your crayons away and line up.
Physical Development: His printing is a little bit messy. He has trouble staying on the line or in the square when he prints.

Share your answer with a classmate or colleague.

3. Learning about children's development and interests

To tailor teaching experiences to meet the developmental needs of individual students, you need to first become familiar with your students. Not only is it important to be aware of your students' development, it is also necessary to know what they find interesting. Although interest as a component of motivation has not been a source of Second Language Acquisition (SLA) research, it is what comes to mind when teachers think of motivation (Cook, 2001). This is especially true of teachers of young learners who are acutely aware that children who are interested and engaged in the specific lesson are less likely to be disruptive. Many experienced teachers are aware that some children who have been diagnosed with attention deficit disorders can attend to an activity for an extended period of time if they find the activity or task to be interesting. By knowing what interests your students, you will be able to create engaging and motivating English lessons.

Action

1. Watch a children's cartoon in English or your native language.
2. Try to determine what age child it is created for as well as whether it is intended more for boys or girls.

Explain to a colleague or classmate how you decided on your answers.

Ways to learn about children's development

There are many ways to learn about children's development and interests. Observing children both in and out of the classroom is a good way to start. You can watch children as they interact with their peers, other teachers, and their parents. By watching their interactions, you are able to look at their development from an emotional and social perspective. The types of conversations that children have can also shed light into their cognitive development. As you watch children play games or engage in sports activities, try to observe their physical development. Are they clumsy or well coordinated? Do they enjoy physical activities or avoid them?

Looking at children and the ways that they interact with their peers both in and out of the classroom can be very informative. It is useful to observe whether children are part of the in-group or whether they are shunned when members of teams are chosen or when children are asked to work with others in pairs or groups. To observe a child's social development, watch how he interacts with his peers and with adults. For example, is he truly interacting with his peers? Is there give and take, or is he being dominated by them? For some children who are shunned, this will be a source of concern, a source of emotional pain, whereas for other children, there will be little concern. Being aware of this aspect of social/emotional development will be helpful when asking children to work with one another.

Children's treasures

Paying attention to children's belongings, the treasures they carry around, is another good way to learn about their interests and development. What children put in their book bags can be a real eye opener. A boy who carries miniature basketballs in his pencil case will most likely have a special interest in basketball. A child who always carries notebooks and pencils with pictures of horses may do so because horses are her favorite animal. A six-year-old who carries and reads books without any pictures has probably developed advanced cognitive skills.

A simple survey

Another way to learn about children's development and interests is by asking them to take simple surveys. Jayne Moon (2002) advocates using surveys as a way to gather information about the learning process from children themselves. Depending on their age, English level, and literacy level, children can answer simple written questions with words and/or pictures.

The reproducible survey on pages 19 and 20 is designed to help you, as a teacher, discover children's perceptions of what they can do both in and out of the classroom. Children are asked to complete sentences about different activities they do at home and school. They are asked specifically to describe what they like to do, what is easy and hard for them to do, as well as who helps them do things which they find to be difficult.

Children who are able to read and write in English can write their responses on the survey. For children who possess literacy skills in their native language, but not in English, you may wish to translate the form into the children's native language. Children who are not able to read and write in English or their native language can dictate their responses to a teacher and draw pictures on the survey.

Obtaining the best results from the survey

Often, when a teacher models a task such as completing an item from the survey, the students merely copy the teacher's example. For instance, if I modeled Number 1 from the survey (At home, I like to _____.) by saying that at home I like to read, all of the students in my class might give the same response. When asking children to give personal or personalized information, it is useful to give an example that they cannot copy so that they will not simply replicate what you have said (Yedlin, 2003). If I provide a model which is impossible for children to replicate, then they are more likely to provide their own content. However, I need to make sure that children are able to understand the language that I use. Therefore, when I give an example, I am careful to use the vocabulary that children have been taught. For example, I might say, "At home, I like to cook dinner for my friends" or "At school, it is hard for me to open the classroom door with my key."

I chose an example from my own life because children enjoy learning about their teachers' real grown-up interests. In the second example, I chose something that my students have observed so that they are more likely to comprehend the example. When I give the second example, I would also show children the classroom door key to help them understand what I am talking about.

| Example 1

5. It used to be hard for me to tie my shoes, but now it is easy.

In Example 1, the response indicates that the child has developed the hand-eye and fine motor skills necessary to tie her own shoes.

Talking to children about their surveys

Not only can you look at children's surveys, you can also talk to them about their responses. It is best to do this on a one-to-one basis when the other children are writing, drawing, or doing other independent work. From both psychological and cultural standpoints, it may not be a good idea to discuss children's responses to the survey in a large group setting. Instead, you can very easily walk around and quietly speak to children about their responses.

Look at Luis's response to Number 10. Seven-year-old Luis has drawn a picture of himself and another boy working together.

Example 2

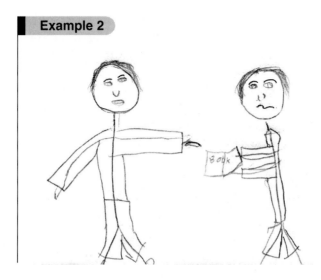

10. I like to have Marco help me when it is hard for me to do something.

In Extract 1, the teacher is able to determine how and why Marco can help. This simple exchange illustrates how Luis understands that he needs extra support and who, among his classmates, can provide that support. As with all extracts in this book, T stands for *teacher* and S stands for *student*.

Extract 1

T: Luis, who can help you at school?

S: Marco.

T: Why do you think Marco can help you at school?

S: Because he is really, really good at spelling, and I'm bad at spelling.

T: Well, spelling may be hard for you, but you are good at drawing.
(Teacher looks and smiles at one of Luis's pictures on the wall.)

S: *Yeah.* (Luis smiles.)

T: *No one can do everything perfectly.* (Luis continues to smile and to look at his picture on the wall.)

Notice the teacher begins the conversation by asking Luis who helps him at school. When Luis states that he is *bad* at spelling, the teacher is careful to mention—in a matter-of-fact way—something that he does well with a concrete example. Children often need to be reminded that what is easy for one person may be very difficult for someone else.

Children's work

Examining children's work, including the drawings and writings that they do on a daily basis, is a good strategy for learning about their growth, development, and interests. Educators and art therapists examine children's drawings in an effort to determine their social/emotional and cognitive development (Levick, 1998). You can look at the facial expressions that children put on the people in their drawings as an indication of their social and emotional development. For instance, I would be concerned when all of the people that a child draws are frowning. Also, children who are younger and less developed cognitively, generally include less detail in their drawings. For example, they may not draw eyebrows or fingers.

Action

Elicit or gather pictures of people drawn by children ages 5 to 12. Examine the emotional expressions on the faces of the people in the pictures. Look at the level of detail of the people. For example, you may want to look at this picture done by a five-year-old girl.

What can you deduce about the child's social, emotional, and cognitive development? Share your deductions with a colleague or classmate.

Talking and Writing Box

Another way to learn about children's interests is by having them create a Talking and Writing Box. The Talking and Writing Box is a small box that children cover with pictures that interest them. They use the box to carry items related to their English-language class. Children create a Talking and Writing Box at the beginning of the year and then use it throughout the year as a basis for speaking and writing activities. In Chapter 3, we will discuss speaking activities that use the Talking and Writing Box. In Chapter 5, you will be given suggestions for writing activities using the Talking and Writing Box.

Materials: A shoe box (or a box the size of a shoebox) for each student, magazines, newspapers and other pictures, scissors, and glue sticks.

Creation of the boxes

1. Have students gather 30–40 pictures that are meaningful to them. Students should be certain to include pictures of food, objects, toys, animals, plants, and people.

2. Have students cut out their pictures and paste them on the outside of their boxes. They first cover the outside of their boxes and then the inside of their boxes.

Figure 4 How to make a Talking and Writing Box

1. Think about your current or potential teaching situation. Consider the students' ages, the number of students in the class, whether the students can read and write in either their native language, English, or both. What are three of the most practical ways to learn about these students' development and interests?

2. What are advantages and disadvantages of each way?

Share your answers with a classmate or colleague.

4. Children's language learning and acquisition

Even though they are related, children's language skills development is separate from their overall development (Freeman and Freeman, 2004). In fact, one of the indicators of cognitive development is language development. Family members, caregivers, and teachers of young learners are acutely aware of the importance of language development.

Krashen (1987) has examined language development and has differentiated the process of **language acquisition** from the process of **language learning**. Language acquisition is the natural process used to develop language skills in a child's native language. The home environment for acquiring a native language is often different from the classroom environment used to teach a second or foreign language. When a child is acquiring their native language at home, the focus is on the message being conveyed rather than the form or correctness of the language. For example, when a native English-speaking child says the word, "Muma" instead of "Mama," her mother would applaud the effort and not worry that the pronunciation was not perfect. When a five-year-old is telling a story about something exciting that took place at camp, his grandmother would focus on what he was talking about rather than how he was saying it.

The term *language learning* is often used to describe the more formal approach to language instruction. Language learning usually refers to the language instruction that takes place in a classroom. Focus is usually on the form of the language rather than on the message being conveyed. For example, in a language-learning classroom, you might see children learning phonics rules–hopefully using a game-format.

It is important to note that even native speakers spend time learning about their language. When it comes to language acquisition and language learning, it doesn't need to be an either-or situation. The focus can be on the message conveyed *and* the form of the language being used.

1. When you were a child between the ages of 5 and 12, what things did you talk about with your family? Did you talk about your favorite doll, toy, or pet? Who did you talk to? Were the conversations mostly focused on form such as correct grammar or meaning?

2. At school, what types of things did you learn about your native language? For example, did you learn about uncommon grammatical constructions?

Share your answers with a classmate or colleague.

5. Making input meaningful to learners

As a teacher, it is important that your students are presented with language that they can understand. **Comprehensible input** is input which is a little bit above the learner's language level but understandable (Krashen, 1986). Although the language is slightly above the learner's level, it is nevertheless meaningful and understandable because of the **context** and other support provided with the input. It is important for you, as a teacher, to provide young learners with different types of input. For example, if you are telling a story about a family, you could use puppets and change your voice as you become each character. You could use a deep voice as you become the father, a higher voice for the mother, and a softer voice for the baby.

As a teacher, there are many different ways that you can make input comprehensible. Here are some suggestions:

- Set the stage. Provide context. For example, if you are going to talk about farm animals, you may want to put up a bulletin board of a scene with pictures of cows, chickens, horses, and other animals.
- Build schema by relating a new topic to the students' prior knowledge and experiences.
- Provide a variety of input. Be sure to provide visual, auditory, and tactile input. Use props, realia, and pictures. Feely boxes (boxes with tactile items inside that children can feel and touch, such as items that are hard, soft, fury, smooth, metal, etc.) and headphones at listening centers are often neglected but good sources of input.
- Make the classroom language rich with environmental print such as labels on the wall, posters with words, and children's books.
- Model each instruction as it is given. Be sure to give only one instruction at a time so that children can directly link the instruction with the actual directions.

- Use language while you are performing different actions. For example, if you are opening a child's thermos, you could say, "I am opening your thermos for you. It is really hard."

1. Think about teaching a lesson on farm animals (cows, donkeys, horses, and chickens) to five-year-old students. Brainstorm ways to make the content comprehensible.
2. How could you introduce the topic?
3. What kinds of visuals could you use? What kinds of sound effects could you use? What kinds of hands-on materials such as toy animals could you use?
4. What type of bulletin board display could you and/or your students make?

6. Supporting children's language acquisition and learning

In addition to making sure that the input is comprehensible, there are many different ways that children's language acquisition and learning can be supported. According to Vygotsky (1978), children's language learning is advanced through social interaction and experiences based on the context or situation. Vygotsky (1962) explains that adults provide children with the language (permanent meanings of words), not with the thinking itself. Nevertheless, adults can support children as learners by modifying interactions to foster both intellectual and language development.

Support can be given to a child within the child's **Zone of Proximal Development (ZPD)** (Vygotsky, 1978). Vygotsky has defined the ZPD as the area of support provided so that a child can accomplish a task she couldn't do on her own. In other words, without that ZPD, a child would be unable to complete a given task independently. Wood, Bruner, and Ross (1978) have used the term "**scaffolding**" to describe the type of support that can be given through interaction within a child's ZPD. The type of scaffolding that is effective is not the same for all cultures and is only effective when it takes into account the child's culture (Berk & Winsler, 1995). In some cultures, a parent or other adult will provide the support necessary for a child to complete a task. In other cultures, it is more likely that a brother or sister, or someone who is closer in age to the child, will provide the support needed to complete the task. Learning this type of information will help you in different ways. For example, it will make it easier for you to advise children who they can go to when they need assistance with homework.

Look at Extract 2 below. Note that the teacher uses the social interaction between herself and her student as a way to provide scaffolding.

This extract is an example of a teacher using her knowledge of her student's interest to provide the scaffolding necessary for the child to answer a question. The teacher is aware that Mi Li may be able to recognize the names of animals even though she may not be able to come up with the words on her own. The teacher also models the language—a complete sentence using Mi Li's information.

The father provides scaffolding for his daughter learning how to walk.

Extract 2

T: Mi Li, what do you like to do on weekends?

S: Play.

T: Who do you like to play with? (Waits a full 10 seconds. Remembers the picture that Mi Li drew playing with her kitten.) *Do you like to play with your dog or your cat?*

S: My cat.

T: Good. You like to play with your cat.

Wait Time

Many teachers make the assumption that when you ask a question you shouldn't wait too long for students to respond or they will get frustrated. Actually the opposite is true. Incorporating **wait time** into your teaching is very important. One way to provide children with support is to increase the amount of time that you wait for them to respond to a question. Sometimes it takes children up to five to ten seconds to access the information being asked for by the teacher.

It is not always necessary for the teacher to provide the scaffold or support for their students. Look back at Extract 1 on page 9. Luis, who is having trouble with phonics, was aware that one of his classmates would be able to help him with spelling. Luis may or may not be aware that the teacher has a lot of other children to help, but in this case he does know who, in addition to the teacher, can provide him with the support.

1. Teachers are not the only people who help children to learn. When you were a child, who, besides your teachers, helped you learn? What did they help you to learn? Think of four people who taught you something when you were a child. For example, my grandmother taught me how to make an omelet.

2. Was the relationship between yourself and the person who helped you important? Why or why not? For instance, was the person a family member? Was he a favorite teacher? What was the relationship like? Was it supportive?

Share your answers with a classmate or colleague.

7. Conclusion

In this chapter, I addressed the issues of younger learners' development and then turned to their language development within the context of overall development. The ways that children develop emotionally, cognitively, and physically were discussed as well as ways to observe children's development and to learn about their interests. I then presented basic concepts related to the development of language skills. Finally, I showed how teachers can use knowledge of the child to make language learning developmentally appropriate.

Further readings

Berk, L.E. and A. Winsler. 1995. *Scaffolding Children's Learning: Vygotsky and Early Childhood Education.* Washington D.C.: NAEYC.

This book helps teachers and caregivers provide young learners with the support (scaffolding) that they need to achieve a wide variety of educational outcomes both large and small.

Tomilinson, C.A. 1999. *The Differentiated Classroom: Responding to the Needs of All Learners.* Alexandria, VA: ASCD (Association for Supervision and Curriculum Development).

This very helpful book provides teachers with practical suggestions for setting up a classroom to meet the developmental needs of all learners.

Walter, T. 1996. *Amazing English: How-To Handbook.* Reading, MA: Addison Wesley.

This book is aimed at teachers of young learners and provides succinct information about second language acquisition. There are numerous charts which help to illustrate some of the most appropriate, child-centered, second language acquisition research.

Helpful Web sites

The Child Development Institute (www.childdevelopmentinfo.com/index.htm)

A helpful web site for teachers and parents interested in learning more about children's development in different areas.

National Association for the Education of Young Children (www.naeyc.org)

This is the web site of the National Association for the Education of Young Children (NAEYC). NAEYC, with 100,000 members, is a professional organization for educators working with young children. NAEYC advocates the use of developmentally appropriate practices and strives to advance the profession of education for young learners.

References

Berk, L.E. and A. Winsler. 1995. *Scaffolding Children's Learning: Vygotsky and Early Childhood Education.* Washington D.C.: NAEYC.

Brazelton, B. and S. Greenspan. 2000. *The Irreducible Needs of Children: What Every Child Must Have to Grow, Learn, and Flourish.* Cambridge, UK: Perseus Publishing.

Cook, V. 1986. *Second Language Learning and Language Teaching. 3rd ed.* New York, NY: Arnold Publishers.

Freeman D. and Y. Freeman. 2004. *Essential Linguistics.* Portsmouth, NH: Heinemann.

Krashen, S.D. 1986. *The Input Hypothesis: Issues and Implications.* London, UK: Longman.

Krashen, S.D. 1987. *Principles and Practice in Second Language Acquisition.* Upper Saddle River, NJ: Prentice-Hall International.

Levick, M. 1998. *See What I'm Saying: What Children Tell Us Through Their Art.* Dubuque, IA: Islewest Publishing.

McClellan D.E. and L.G. Katz. *Assessing Children's Social Competence.* [updated 2001; cited 31 March 2005]. Available from http://vtaide.com/png/ERIC/Social-Competence-Checklist.htm.

Moon, J. 2000. *Children Learning English.* Oxford, UK: Macmillan Education.

Nurturing Social Emotional Development of Gifted Children (n.d.) [cited 31 March 2005]. Available from http://www.mental-health-matters.com/articles/article.php?artID=398

Vygotsky, L. 1978. *Mind and Society: The development of higher psychological processes.* (M. Cole, V. John-Steiner, S. Scribner, eds. and trans.) Cambridge, MA: Harvard University Press.

Vygotsky, L. 1962. *Thought and Language.* (A. Kouzin trans.) Cambridge, MA: MIT Press.

Wood D. J., J.S. Bruner, and G. Ross. 1976. The role of tutoring in problem solving. *Journal of Child Psychology and Psychiatry,* 1976(17): 89–100.

Yedlin, J. 2003. *Teacher talk and writing development in an urban, English-as-a-second-language, first-grade classroom.* Cambridge, MA: Unpublished doctoral dissertation Harvard Graduate School of Education.

Name: _____   Date: _____

Complete each sentence. Draw a picture to go with each sentence.

At Home	**At School**
1. I like to _____.	**2.** I like to _____.
3. It is easy for me to _____.	**4.** It is easy for me to _____.
5. It is hard for me to _____.	**6.** It is hard for me to _____.

(continued)

Name: _____   Date: _____

Complete each sentence. Draw a picture to go with each sentence.

At Home	**At School**

7. It used to be hard for me to_____, but now it easy.	**8.** It used to be hard for me to_____, but now it is easy.
9. I like to have _____ help me when it is hard for me to do something.	**10.** I like to have _____ help me when it is hard for me to do something.

Chapter **Two**

Teaching listening to young learners

Goals

At the end of this chapter, you should be able to:

✔ **define** listening as it relates to children.

✔ **describe** different learning channels.

✔ **list** examples of the types of listening skills that young learners need to have.

✔ **explain** how Total Physical Response (TPR) helps students with different learning channels develop listening skills.

✔ **identify** listening activities for children learning English as a foreign or second language.

1. Introduction

In this chapter, we will discuss listening and the teaching of listening as it pertains to young learners. In the next section, listening is described and contrasted with hearing. A background for the teaching of listening is then presented with an emphasis on the three learning channels. Listening as a foundation skill for other skills is described next. We end the chapter with a variety of classroom techniques and activities which can be used with students at differing stages of language and literacy acquisition.

2. What is listening?

Babies as young as one and two months of age have the capacity to discriminate speech sounds (Vihman, 1996). Before babies can comprehend words, they listen to the rhythm and melody of the language and have some awareness of interaction and relationship with a speaker (Cook, 2000). Toddlers listen to both sounds and words. Eventually, children start tuning in to words and the meanings attached to them. For example, a very young child will quickly learn the meaning of the word "No!" when she gets too close to something hot on the stove.

Listening versus hearing

Hearing is different from listening. Hearing refers to the actual perception and processing of sound. In order to be able to listen in class, children need to be able to hear. It has been reported that up to 18% of children in some countries have hearing loss before they are 19 years of age. Even minor hearing loss can have a very profound impact on a child's ability to listen and fully participate in the English-language classroom.

When a child is learning her native language, family members are able to **scaffold** and adjust the linguistic input that the child receives. For example, a father might speak more loudly or slowly. The father may not even realize that he is making adjustments because of hearing loss. In a classroom setting, this is much harder to do but not impossible. Figure 1 (page 23) lists indicators teachers can look for to determine if a child might have a hearing problem.

The child:

pulls on ear.

has frequent ear infections.

complains of ear aches.

complains of ringing in the ear.

asks for the CD or tape player to be turned up when the volume seems to be fine for everyone else.

asks for things to be repeated even when said in the child's native language.

has trouble repeating words and phrases.

Figure 1 Indicators of possible hearing loss

There are different ways that you can help children with hearing loss. As a teacher, you can place a child who has a hearing loss in the front of the classroom so that he can see your lips move and is in your direct line of sound. You can also make sure that he doesn't sit next to children who are noisy because that can muffle out your voice or the voice of a CD or cassette.

What children listen to

Young children listen to a variety of voices and sounds that are around them. Inside buildings, they may hear people talking, a television, a vacuum cleaner, pots banging, or a microwave oven. Children often announce when they suddenly hear a specific outdoor sound such as a fire engine or an ambulance. If children live in an area where there are animals, they learn to distinguish the sounds of dogs barking, cows mooing, sheep baaing, etc. Young learners also enjoy listening to songs and stories.

In the box below, write four sounds that children in your community hear. Include sounds that are heard inside as well as those heard outside. Include everyday sounds such as water boiling or dogs barking. Then list the English-language topics that correspond to each sound to create a chart like the one below.

Sound	Young Learner Topic
water boiling	cooking, kitchen
dog barking	animals, pets

Share your answer with a classmate or colleague.

Let me point out that there are few things more enchanting for a child than to eavesdrop on conversations they believe are only intended for grown-ups. Experienced teachers and parents know that a good way to capture children's attention is to talk to another adult and pretend that the children aren't present. If a beginning teacher is having trouble controlling an unruly class, a good strategy is to bring another adult into the doorway of the classroom. Then the teacher should talk about the unruly class as if they weren't even there. Rest assured that the class will actively listen to the conversation and any suggestions that either adult gives.

Listening as one of the four language skills

When we talk about language learning, we often talk about the four language skills: listening, speaking, reading, and writing. We can further distinguish the skills by stating that listening and speaking are oral skills while reading and writing are written skills. We can also distinguish between the skills and their direction. Listening and reading are **receptive** skills because the focus is on receiving information from an outside source. Speaking and writing, on the other hand, are **productive** skills because the focus is on producing information.

Some people think that because children do not need to produce sounds when they are listening, that listening is passive. But this is not true. Learners can and should be actively engaged in listening tasks and activities. As we will see later in this chapter, there are many ways that children can be actively involved in listening activities and still have their mouths closed.

Listening as a foundation for other skills

The relationship between listening and speaking is clear because they are both oral skills. By listening, children are preparing to replicate the sounds when they speak. In addition, as we will see on page 28, there are specific listening skills which can lay the foundation for reading instruction because by developing good listening skills, children are able to match the sounds with the corresponding symbols when they **decode** words. In addition, listening comprehension skills can prepare children to develop reading comprehension skills.

3. Background to the teaching of listening

Learning channels are the preferred ways that learners receive and process information. Most learners favor one style more than the others. As a teacher of young learners, you need to be familiar with the three main learning channels which are **auditory, tactile,** and **visual.** In general, auditory learners are better able to learn material when it is presented in an auditory format such as listening to someone read a story aloud. Visual learners often recall visual images or pictures easily. Tactile learners are better able to remember information, language, and content when they have physically manipulated or touched the information. Tactile learners benefit when they have actually made something with their hands.

Think of children listening to a picture storybook being read aloud. The visual learners will not be satisfied unless they have a good view of the pictures. The truly auditory learners will be content to listen to the words and the tale being told with only the minimal amount of visual input or pictures. The tactile learners will want to have puppets or other props that they can handle as they listen to the story being told or as they tell the story themselves.

Look at Figure 2 (page 26) to see the types of input which can be provided for the different learning channels.

Learning Channels	Examples of Input
Auditory	Songs, chants, poems, stories read aloud, environmental sounds such as rain, cars, trucks, animals, vacuum cleaners, computer printers, people walking
Visual	Pictures such as drawings, sketches, photographs, paintings, posters, murals, diagrams
Tactile	Real life objects that children can touch as well as toys and puppets (It is important to make sure that the child can actually touch the objects and not merely look at them.)

Figure 2 Types of input for different learning channels

In order to make the language comprehensible to all learners, you should try to present information using all three learning channels. As noted earlier, all learners use a combination of different learning channels even though they may have a preference for one over the others. The majority of learners prefer visual input although it should be noted that babies tend to be more auditory and only develop a preference for other channels later on at different times depending upon their development.

Keep in mind that teachers have a tendency to teach to their own preference. So it is very important that you are aware of your own channel preference so that you can make more of an effort to teach to children who have different preferences.

For example, I am an auditory learner, so I prefer to give instructions aloud rather than to write them on the board. I have to remind myself to write out the instructions for my visual learners.

1. In the chart below, write five songs and stories that children listen to. You may want to look at Appendix 1, Children's Songs and Finger-plays on pages 204–208.
2. Think of the type of input that you could give to make each song or story comprehensible to learners with different learning channels. Write them in the chart.

Story or Song	Visual Learners	Auditory Learners	Tactile Learners
Row, Row, Row Your Boat	Pictures of row boats and rivers	Environmental sounds of a river	Rowing motions

Compare your answers with a classmate or colleague.

4. The development of listening skills

Teachers of young learners know the importance of teaching children how to listen. This is true for both a first-language and second- or foreign-language classroom. As teachers of **second-** and **foreign-language learners**, it is useful to consider the listening skills that are taught to children learning English as a first language. For example, a five-year-old native speaker who is not able to listen to and follow simple instructions is probably not going to be ready to learn academic content such as colors, numbers, shapes, days of the week, letters, and sounds. The same holds true for the non-native student. Being able to follow simple instructions is one of the foundation listening **readiness skills** that get children ready to develop other language skills. The following statements help to summarize how other skills are built on listening.

You need to hear a word before you can say it.
You need to say a word before you can read it.
You need to read a word before you can write it.

Listening skills also help children who have literacy skills in their own language transition into English-language literacy. Look at Figure 3 to see how the development of different listening skills helps children get ready to read. Listening skills prepare children for reading in their native language as well as reading in a second or foreign language.

Skill	How it Prepares for Reading
1. Listens to and follows instructions such as *Take out your pencil and your green activity book*	Prepares children for a variety of academic tasks
2. Can follow an oral sequence of events such as *Lucy went to the refrigerator and took out some milk*	Prepares children to comprehend stories
3. Can listen attentively to stories	Prepares children to comprehend stories
4. Can comprehend a story that has been read and/or told	Prepares children to comprehend stories
5. Can discriminate between sound such as /b/ and /p/	Prepares children to decode words / Helps to prepare children for phonics instruction
6. Can identify rhyming sounds	Prepares children to decode words / Helps to prepare children for phonics instruction
7. Can segment (or separate) words into syllables such as *ap-ple* or *din-ner*	Prepares children to decode words / Helps to prepare children for phonics instruction

Figure 3 Listening skills for young learners

Listening skills to prepare children to read

When a teacher shares a story with children and helps them to develop listening comprehension skills, she is also working on their reading readiness skills. Listening comprehension utilizes many of the same processes necessary to read and comprehend a story (Piper, 1993). **Listening capacity** refers to an informal measure of one's ability to understand or comprehend spoken language in the context of a story being told or read aloud (Gunning 2003, 2000). As a foundation for reading, we need to develop children's listening comprehension and listening capacity.

Children who can segment words and listen to isolated sounds have developed **phonological awareness**. Phonological awareness refers to the ability to listen and think about the entire range of sounds that occur in a word (Heilman, 2002). For example, words are made up of phonemes—individual sounds—as well as syllables. By developing listening skills that focus on phonological awareness, children will be better prepared to participate in phonics instruction which, in turn, will make it easier for them to decode and read words. For more information about phonics instruction see Chapter 4.

If children have been trained to carefully listen to English-language sounds, they will be in a much better position to match the sound with a specific letter or symbol. Consequently, if children haven't developed phonological awareness, they can be very confused when they begin reading instruction. For instance, if children have trouble discriminating /r/ and /l/, they could have trouble with a phonics lesson focused on these sounds. It is much easier to learn how to listen to sounds first and then only later add the print.

Auditory patterns

Another way to think about the relationship between listening and reading is to consider the fact that one needs to recognize patterns in order to read. Reading is about patterns. Detecting the auditory or phonological patterns that occur in language will better prepare children for the visual patterns that occur in English-language words. In English, unlike some other languages, there are many single syllable words that rhyme. Rhymes are an important component of many English-language songs, finger-plays, and chants for children. By learning to recognize rhyming words, children will be in a better position to decode and read words that follow a similar pattern.

5.   Classroom techniques and activities

As a teacher working with children learning **English as a second language (ESL)** or **English as a foreign language (EFL),** I try to blend techniques designed for ESL or EFL learners with those intended for young children learning English as their first language. I sometimes use approaches which are designed for adult EFL learners and adapt them when necessary so that they will be appropriate for young learners. I also draw upon techniques which are designed for native English speakers and adapt them for the ESL or EFL classroom. Like Paul (2003), I feel that it is important to provide specific activities which give children listening practice.

Total Physical Response (TPR) activities

James J. Asher (1977) studied the way very young children acquire language. Asher wondered why very young children were so good at developing language skills when students in college and university classes had so much difficulty. He observed that babies spent the first year of their life just listening to language. He noticed that although infants aren't speaking, they are still active users of the language because they are physically responding to what has been said.

Young learners can listen and follow simple commands.

Asher took his findings and developed a method which is known as **Total Physical Response (TPR)**. Learners *physically* respond to oral commands which are given. Just as with babies, learners are expected to respond non-verbally to commands before they are expected to speak. The teacher usually gives an oral command while she demonstrates it. For example, she may jump while she says the word *jump*. After watching, children begin to respond physically when they hear the word *jump* by jumping. The learners follow along with the commands and only speak when they are ready. When they first begin to speak, they repeat the commands given by the teacher.

TPR has several positive aspects. First, it utilizes the auditory, visual, and tactile learning channels. The learners listen and watch as the commands are given. Later, the learners have a chance to use all three channels: they listen, watch one another, and do the commands themselves. Second, TPR helps to teach children to follow directions and listen attentively—two important skills for academic success. Third, in keeping with developmentally appropriate notions or thoughts, children are allowed to listen and then choose when they feel comfortable to start speaking. Fourth, this method can easily be adapted in many different ways for young learners.

There are many different ways that TPR can be used with young learners. For children who are just beginning to study English, a variety of simple one-word commands, such as *jump, stand, wave, wiggle* can be used.

Gradually, more complicated child-friendly commands can be introduced.

Example 1

These children are enjoying a TPR activity.

Whenever putting together a TPR activity, it is important to consider the complexity of the language being used as well as the interest level of the children. I think about the vocabulary that I am going to use and if the words are too difficult or too simple. I try to make sure that the grammar is clear and easily illustrated with the commands. I also think about and bring to class props, real objects, or pictures which will make the activity appealing to both visual and tactile learners.

Action

1. Make a list of three different types of sequences that take place in a typical home. For example, *setting the table, making a bed, washing the dishes.*
2. Write a set of commands with the language that you would use to carry out each sequence. For example, the following instructions for setting the table could be written for seven-year-olds who are at the beginning stages of English-language development:
   Open the drawer.
   Take out the chopsticks.
   Carry the chopsticks over to the table.
   Put the chopsticks on the table.

Compare your answers with a classmate or colleague.

When using TPR with five-, six-, or seven-year-olds, be sure to give only one command at a time. As a teacher of young learners, you need to be aware that some children, especially five-, six-, or seven-year-olds, will have trouble paying attention to multi-step instructions due to their overall development. By waiting until everyone has followed the one instruction which has been given, you are better able to keep instructions in the target language. The children are able to more easily link that instructional language with the action. If you give more than one instruction at a time, it can be difficult to figure out if the children are not following along because they don't understand the language being spoken or if they lost track of what it is they are supposed to do. By giving TPR commands one at a time, you are able to look around the room to determine if the children are comprehending what you are saying in an instant.

TPR songs and finger-plays

TPR can be used with songs and **finger-plays** (See Appendix 1). Finger-plays are little chants that children say while moving their fingers and/or hands. One of the most popular finger-plays is "The Eensy Weensy Spider" (Example 2). As children say the finger-play, they pantomime the spider climbing up the spout.

Example 2

The Eensy Weensy Spider

The eensy weensy spider climbed up the water spout.

Down came the rain and washed the spider out.

Out came the sun and dried up all the rain.

And the eensy weensy spider climbed up the spout again.

Example 3 is another example of a popular finger-play. At first, you chant the finger-play as the children use their hands and their fingers to point to the correct body parts. After they understand the chant, the children can chant and point the finger-play.

Example 3

Head and Shoulders

Head and shoulders, knees and toes, knees and toes,

Head and shoulders, knees and toes, knees and toes,

Eyes and ears and mouth and nose,

Head and shoulders, knees and toes, knees and toes.

When adding hand signals and gestures to songs and finger-plays, be sure to use ones that are meaningful to children and show them what they mean. For instance, if you have children row a boat, you will either want to draw a picture of a rowboat on the board or show them a picture of a rowboat. Children may delight in creating their own hand signals such as their own way of rowing a boat "merrily."

TPR storytelling

TPR can also be used in conjunction with storytelling. It works especially well with stories where sentence patterns are repeated. I choose a favorite story such as "Goldilocks and the Three Bears" and tell it using puppets or storytelling pieces. Storytelling pieces are pictures of characters and different items in a story that children manipulate or move around as the story is told. Example 4 (page 34) is a set of reproducible storytelling pieces, and Example 5 (pages 34–35) is the text of the story. Using pictures, I introduce the difficult vocabulary items prior to telling the story. I tell the story as I manipulate the puppets or storytelling pieces. Next, I invite volunteers to hold different puppets or storytelling pieces and move them appropriately as they are mentioned in the story. When children are even more familiar with the story, I provide each of them with their own copies of the storytelling pieces. Children hold up the corresponding storytelling piece as I tell the story. I am aware that when I do this I must slow down the telling or reading of the story so that all of the children can keep up. Eventually, I invite children to be guest storytellers and to have them tell parts of the story while the others hold up the matching pieces.

Example 4

Papa Bear	Mama Bear	Baby Bear
Papa's bowl	Mama's bowl	Baby's bowl
Papa's chair	Mama's chair	Baby's chair
Papa's bed	Mama's bed	Baby's bed
Goldilocks	Door to the Bear's house	Bear house

Example 5

Goldilocks and the Three Bears

Once upon a time, there were three bears. There was Mama Bear. There was Papa Bear. There was Baby Bear. They all lived in a house in the woods. One day, Mama Bear made some porridge. Mama Bear put the porridge on the table for the three bears.

The three bears wanted the porridge to cool off. The three bears went for a walk. While they were gone, Goldilocks walked by the bears' house. Goldilocks looked into the window. Goldilocks opened the door. She walked inside. She saw the porridge on the table.

Goldilocks ate some of Papa Bear's porridge. She said, "This porridge is too hot." She ate some of Mama Bear's porridge. She said, "This porridge is too cold." She ate some of Baby Bear's porridge. She said, "This porridge is just right." And she ate it all up.

Next, Goldilocks went into the living room. She sat in Papa Bear's chair. She said, "This chair is too hard." Next, she sat in Mama Bear's chair. She said, "This chair is too soft." Next, she sat in Baby Bear's chair. She said, "This chair is just right." She sat in Baby Bear's chair and it broke.

Next, Goldilocks went into the bedroom. She lay down in Papa Bear's bed. She said, "This bed is too hard." Next, she lay down in Mama Bear's bed. She said, "This bed is too soft." Next, she lay down in Baby Bear's bed. She said, "This bed is just right." She lay down in Baby Bear's bed and fell asleep.

The three bears came home. Papa Bear said, "Someone ate my porridge." Mama Bear said, "Someone ate my porridge." Baby Bear said, "Someone ate my porridge all up." The three bears went into the living room. Papa Bear said, "Someone sat in my chair." Mama Bear said, "Someone sat in my chair." Baby Bear said, "Someone sat in my chair and broke it."

The three bears went into the bedroom. Papa Bear said, "Someone lay down on my bed." Mama Bear said, "Someone lay down on my bed." Baby Bear said, "Someone lay down on my bed and here she is."

Goldilocks got up and ran away.

Reflection

1. Count the number of times that different sentence patterns are repeated. For example, "This porridge is too _____" is repeated three times.

2. Why would repeating sentence patterns help young learners?

Share your answers with a classmate or colleague.

Action

1. Make a list of five different children's stories.
2. Choose one story that you know well enough to tell to children. Make sure the story contains repeated sentence patterns.
3. Make a script for the story and a list of the story-telling pieces that you would need.

Share your story with a classmate or colleague.

Yes/no cards

By using TPR *yes/no* cards, you can easily measure children's listening capacity. When using *yes/no* cards, children are asked questions and then respond by showing a yes or no card. Figure 4 has instructions for making *yes/no* cards.

1. Provide children with two index cards which are large enough for the teacher to see from the front of the classroom.
2. Children make one card with a happy face and the word *yes* on both the front and back.
3. Children make a second card with a sad face and the word *no* on both the front and back.

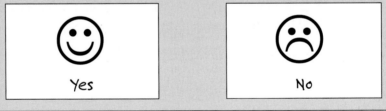

Figure 4 How to make *yes/no* cards

Traditionally, when children have been asked questions orally, they also respond orally. The teacher might ask one student a question while everyone else in the class sits and listens. For a couple of students this strategy works well, but if you ask every student in my class a question and wait for all of them to respond, you have given them too much of an opportunity to fidget and become disruptive. In other cases, you can ask the question of the entire class and wait for them to respond in unison. The problem with this second approach is that the answer may be very noisy and it could be hard to determine who was and was not responding correctly. The use of *yes/no* cards alleviates or eliminates this problem because children show their answers silently rather than tell their answers in unison verbally.

It is important to print the word *yes* on the front and back of the card so that when children are holding up the card they see the same signal for *yes* as you do. *Yes/no* cards are a wonderful way to check comprehension throughout the English-language lesson. The happy and sad faces work well with children who are five and six years old and do not yet possess literacy skills in English.

In an effort to minimize children waving the cards around, I show children how to place the cards on their chest. I always make sure that children are seated in such a way that I can see all of their cards. In smaller classrooms, you may want to have some children sitting on the floor and others sitting in chairs behind them, so that all of the cards are visible to you.

Extract 1 demonstrates how you can use *yes/no* cards with a story. As with all extracts in the book, T stands for *teacher* and Ss stands for *students*.

Extract 1

T: *Was Goldilocks a girl?*
Ss: (Some hold up *yes* cards and others *no* cards.)
T: (Notices that several children are holding the *no* card instead of the *yes* card. The teacher then holds up the picture of Goldilocks and asks the question again.) *Was Goldilocks a girl?*
Ss: (All are holding up the *yes* card.)
T: *Yes, Goldilocks was a girl.*

As a teacher, you can look around and see how many children were able to comprehend the question and answer it correctly. You can then adjust your questioning to meet the needs of the learners in the classroom by making the subsequent questions easier or more difficult. Another advantage to using *yes/no* cards is that the adjustment to instruction can take place instantaneously unlike written assignments where it is necessary to wait and look at everyone's work before adjusting the language level and questioning level to meet the needs of the learners.

Make the language simple when checking comprehension

When checking comprehension of a story, song, or finger-play, I try to use constructions which are simple. If I use a complicated construction such as, *Didn't Goldilocks break the chair?* and the children get the answer wrong, I am not sure if they are having difficulty with the grammatical construction of the question or whether they are having difficulty with the actual content of the story itself. Instead, I am careful to ask a simple yes/no question: *Did Goldilocks break the chair?*

TPR drawing

One activity that children enjoy doing is following TPR drawing instructions. All of the children can be given the same instructions but should be given latitude in how they carry out the instructions. For instance, you might give the following commands:

1. Draw a circle.
2. Draw two eyes. The eyes can be any color you want.
3. Draw some hair. Make it long or short.

Syllable clapping

There are a number of ways to help children become more aware of auditory patterns that occur in language. As mentioned earlier, giving children a good phonological awareness foundation prepares them to engage in beginning formal reading instruction. One way to help children learn the way that words are broken into syllables and into separate words is to chant the words while you clap them in syllables. For example, for the two-syllable word *happy*, you would clap when you say *hap-* and you would clap again when you say *-py*. This is useful for the tactile learners as well as auditory learners. To make this more accessible to the visual learner, you may want to show pictures of the words being clapped. If you are clapping adjectives such as *happy* or *angry*, you may want to invite volunteers to demonstrate being *happy* or *angry* as the rest of the children clap and chant the words.

Rhyming word activities

I tend to be cautious using rhyming words in the ESL or EFL classroom. Although rhymes are wonderful and are especially useful in the forms of finger-plays and songs, the language is not always completely accessible for children. Figure 5 has words which are frequently used to reinforce the concept of rhyming words with native English speakers. Notice the number of words which are somewhat uncommon and not used in frequent communication. For a native English speaker or even for children learning English as a second language in an English-speaking environment, these words can be learned relatively easily. However, for children learning English as a foreign language these words can be very challenging.

fat	vat	cat	hat	bat
mat	sat	rat	Nat	pat

Underlined words are uncommon or infrequently used.

Figure 5 Rhyming words

1. Make a list of seven words that rhyme with *man*.
2. Make lists of seven words that rhyme with *sit* and *line*.
3. Circle the words that would be appropriate to teach children who are at the beginning stages of learning English. Draw a square around the words that would be appropriate for children eight and under.
4. Notice how many words are inappropriate to teach a child who is learning English.

Share your list with a classmate or colleague.

Minimal pairs

In order to discern or figure out auditory patterns, children must be aware of similarities and differences in words. **Minimal pairs** are two words that differ in only one sound. For example, *bat* and *pat* are minimal pairs. One way to practice minimal pair distinction is to have your learners listen to two words and tell whether they are the same or different by holding up the *yes/no* cards. For example, students might have to discriminate between *b* and *p* or between the short *i* and long *e* sounds. Murphy (2003) suggests the use of pictures to make the traditional technique known as minimal pairs more meaningful. For example, if you are doing a minimal pair with the following words you might want to include picture cards (Example 6).

Example 6

ship

sheep

6. Listening in the classroom

Most children's coursebooks include listening activities where children listen and do something. For the activity in Example 7, the children listen as the teacher reads the script or plays the audio recording and writes the numeral for the corresponding picture.

Example 7

Kid's Safari 2 (Greenwell, 2002, p. 36)

Once the activities given in the book are completed, many of these pages can be reused by giving an additional set of drawing instructions. For example:

1. Draw chocolate milk in the cup.
2. Draw a piece of carrot on the fork.
3. Draw orange juice in the glass.
4. Draw a fish on the plate.
5. Draw an apple next to the knife.
6. Draw some soup on the spoon.

Action

Look at a listening activity from a young learners' coursebook. Focus on a listening book page that has very little print. Discuss how it can be used two different ways. One should be the way that it is used in the coursebook. The second way should be of your own invention.

Share your answers with your classmates or colleagues.

There are also coursebooks that incorporate listening with reading. Students, for example, may listen to a passage and then answer questions that they hear on an audio recording or read aloud. Look at Example 8 (page 42) from a coursebook designed for nine-year-olds who have English-language literacy skills and have studied English for several years. It is important to make sure that the students have the literacy skills to do the exercise. For example, students would have to be able to read the irregular spelling pattern *ph* for the sound /f/ in order to recognize the word *dolphin*. You could very easily adapt this page into an activity that only involved listening by having students hold up the *yes/no* cards while you read the questions aloud.

Example 8

1 Listen and choose *yes* or *no*.

FACT SHEET: Dolphin Girl		
run very fast	yes	no
swim very fast	yes	no
fly	yes	no
lift a car	yes	no
climb walls	yes	no
jump over houses	yes	no

2 Complete using *can* or *can't*.

Dolphin Girl _____ run very fast and she _____ swim very fast.

She _____ fly. She _____ lift a car. She _____ climb walls and

she _____ jump over houses.

3 Invent a superhero. Write *yes* or *no* in the fact sheet.

FACT SHEET: _____	
run very fast	
swim very fast	
fly	
lift a car	
climb walls	
jump over houses	

4 Draw and talk about your superhero.

Monkey Boy can climb walls. He can't swim very fast.

All Aboard 2 (Davies, 2004, p. 45)

7. Conclusion

In this chapter, I contrasted listening with hearing and discussed the development of listening skills. Some of the links between the development of listening skills and reading skills were presented. In this chapter, I also showed how young children can be actively engaged in a language class even without speaking. A variety of suggestions for teaching listening skills in the L2 classroom were provided including a variety of adaptations for using Total Physical Response with children at differing stages of language development.

Further readings

Geller, K. 2001. *Follow the Directions and Draw it All by Yourself.* New York, NY: Scholastic Books.

This teacher resource book provides a host of learning tasks and activities for children. By listening and following the directions, children create lovely pictures.

Seeley, C. and E. Romijin 1991. *TPR Is More than Commands – At All Levels.* Berkeley, CA: Command Performance Language Institute.

This charming teacher resource book is filled with ideas for using TPR in a wide variety of contexts. Although the activities are designed primarily for teaching older learners, they can very easily be adapted for working with children.

Helpful Web site

Alexander Graham Bell Association for the Deaf and Hard of Hearing (www.agbell.org)

This site provides information about hearing loss. It includes information for parents who are concerned that their child may suffer from hearing loss as well as for teachers working with children who are hearing impaired.

References

Asher, J. J. 1977. *Learning Another Language Through Actions: The Complete Teacher's Guide Book*. Los Gatos, CA: Sky Oaks Productions.

Cook, G. 2000. *Language Play, Language Learning*. Oxford, UK: Oxford University Press.

Davies, P. 2004. *All Aboard! 2*. Oxford, UK: Macmillan Educational Publishers.

Greenwell, J. 2003. *Kid's Safari*. New York, NY: McGraw-Hill.

Gunning, T. 2003, 2000. *Creating Literacy Instruction for All Children*. Boston, MA: Allyn and Bacon.

Heilman, A. W. 2002. *Phonics in Proper Perspective. 9th ed*. Upper Saddle River, NJ: Merrill-Prentice Hall.

Murphy, J. 2003. Pronunciation. In D. Nunan (ed.), *Practical English Language Teaching*. New York, NY: McGraw-Hill, 111–128.

Paul, D. 2003. *Teaching English to Children in Asia*. Hong Kong, PRC: Longman Asia ELT.

Piper, T. 1993. *Language for All Our Children*. New York, NY: Merrill (Imprint of Macmillian).

Vihman, M. 1996. *Phonological Development: The Origins of Language in the Child*. Cambridge, MA: Blackwell Publishers.

Chapter **Three**

Teaching speaking to young learners

Goals

At the end of this chapter, you should be able to:

✔ **define** speaking as it relates to children.

✔ **identify** expectations for children's oral language use and development.

✔ **explain** the advantages and disadvantages of the Audiolingual Method and Communicative Language Teaching for young learners.

✔ **describe** the role of pronunciation in a young learner's speaking program.

✔ **discuss** ways to correct young learners' errors.

✔ **describe** some of the challenges of using speaking activities with young learners.

✔ **demonstrate** familiarity with the techniques discussed in this chapter.

1. Introduction

This chapter begins with a description of speaking and the role of speaking in children's development of their first language. Background information on the teaching of speaking is provided. Next, an explanation of the development of speaking skills is provided including specific issues that you will encounter in the classroom. This is followed by a number of different techniques and activities which you can use with young learners. Suggestions for managing the noise level in the classroom are also presented.

2. What is speaking?

There are many different ways that children play with words and language beginning with the tickling rhymes that they hear as babies and continuing with other sorts of play which involve both the form and meaning of language (Cook, 2000). When children begin speaking, they experiment and play with the **utterances** that are made to form words and phrases such as *bye-bye*, or *go bye-bye*. As they grow, children integrate these words and structures into their real and imaginary play. Play is a vital and important aspect of a child's development and language is a part of that play. It is important to consider the role of play in first language acquisition because it is a subtle reminder that play is also important in children's second language development. This reminder is useful when we plan **ESL** and **EFL** activities that foster children's English-language development.

The mother is helping her son expand his vocabulary.

It is also good to remember that children experiment with their native language when they are with their parents, other caregivers, siblings, and friends. This trying out of different words and phrases leads a native English-speaking child to acquire a 10,000-word vocabulary by the time he is four. In addition, very early on, children learn the power of their spoken words. They learn that, although they may be physically small and weak, their words can be used to provide joy. A child learns that a simple utterance such as *Mommy, I love you* can delight a parent.

On the other hand, young children may use words as a weapon against one another causing hurt feelings and bruised egos. In an attempt to deflect some of the power of words that children hurl at one another, native English-speaking children are often taught the following rhyme:

Sticks and stones
will break my bones,
but words will never hurt me.

Children also learn that words can be used as a form of entertainment. Children talk while they play, either alone or with their classmates. During playtime at school or home, you might see children **role-playing.** They practice conversations between one another. In their play, they practice and adapt scripts that they have heard from adults either in person or on TV. Young children talk when they engage in make-believe activities. For example, a five-year-old girl might enjoy giving royal commands as she struts around the house with a plastic crown pretending that she is the finest princess in all the land. Young learners who are 10 and 11 years old do not engage in as much "pretending" as children who are slightly younger; however, they still enjoy dressing up for Halloween—a North American holiday where children dress in costumes and go door to door asking for candy. The children may try to talk the way a princess or a firefighter talks depending upon the costume being worn. Ten- and 11-year-olds are more likely to become interested in a different type of make-believe, such as science fiction.

Reflection

What do young children in your country like to pretend to be? For example, kings, queens, police officers, teachers. When you were a child, what did you like to pretend to be? What were some of the things that you might have said when you were playing? What would you have said when you were five? What would you have said when you were 10?

Share your answers with a classmate or colleague.

3. Background to the teaching of speaking

In Chapter 2, the role that listening plays in children's language development was discussed. Speaking is equally important in children's overall language development. Children learning English as their native language spend time developing speaking skills. If you were to visit a class for native English-speaking five-year-olds in North America, you would undoubtedly see children saying **finger-plays**, simple chants and rhymes with hand or finger motions. They would also be singing songs with their teacher. Usually the entire class sits together while everyone sings or chants in unison. This is a regular and important part of the school day because teachers working with young learners recognize how important it is for children to develop strong speaking skills.

Many of the songs and finger-plays that children learn to say contain language that is repetitive. Look at Example 1—two favorite children's songs—and see how much repetition there is in each song. Both of these songs also lend themselves to pantomime and TPR-style activities (see page 30). Children can easily mime the actions until they feel comfortable saying the words. Children gradually learn the repetitive lyrics of songs and eventually the entire songs.

Example 1

This is the way we wash our clothes
This is the way we wash our clothes, wash our clothes, wash our clothes.
This is the way we wash our clothes so early Monday morning.
This is the way we iron our clothes, iron our clothes, iron our clothes.
This is the way we iron our clothes so early Tuesday morning.

The Hokey-Pokey
You put your right foot in.
You put your right foot out.
You put your right foot in.
You shake it all about.
You do the Hokey-Pokey and you turn yourself around.
That's what it's all about.
You put your left foot in.
(Etc.)

Children can make up their own verses or versions of songs and finger-plays known as **innovations**. This gives children an opportunity to take a known pattern and put their own twist to it. Teachers prompt children in order to come up with their own verses (see Figure 1).

You put your left elbow in.
You put your left elbow out.
You put your left elbow in.
You shake it all about.
You do the Hokey-Pokey and you turn yourself around.
That's what it's all about!

You put your left ear in.
You put your left ear out.
You put your left ear in.
You shake it all about.
You do the Hokey-Pokey and you turn yourself around.
That's what it's all about!

Figure 1 An innovation of *The Hokey-Pokey*

Once children understand how to create their own verses, they often can be found on the playground making up all sorts of verses for different songs.

4. The development of speaking skills

Contrary to popular myth, younger children learning English as a foreign language do not develop English-language skills more readily than older learners. However, they have a clear advantage when it comes to pronunciation if they begin learning English as a foreign or second language at an early age (Birdsong, 1999). Nevertheless, there are some phonemes which English-speaking as well as non-native-speaking children have difficulty with. It is not uncommon for a six-year-old child to have trouble articulating /r/. The /s/ sound as well as /th/ can also be difficult for some children. As a teacher working with ESL or EFL, you should keep this in mind when you are working on pronunciation. I do not focus too much on sounds that are troublesome for children until they are 10 or 11 years old, and even then I am careful not to insist.

I am also very careful to look at children's mouths when they are having trouble pronouncing different sounds. Sometimes the cause of difficulty can be as simple as baby teeth that have fallen out and are not yet replaced by adult teeth. Or a child may have just received dental braces or a dental retainer and may be slightly struggling with different phonemes because of this.

Avoid unrealistic expectations

What is known about the development of English-language skills in native English-speaking children can be used to influence the way that we teach English to ESL or EFL young learners. The expectations for children learning ESL or EFL should not be greater or more demanding than the expectations for children learning to speak in English as their native language. When working with children learning ESL or EFL, I try to keep in mind some of the issues that impact native English speakers and make sure that my expectations are not unrealistic. The two issues that I am most concerned with are mean length of utterances and pronunciation and are described below.

Mean length of utterances

Educators and linguists examining native-English language development look at the child's **mean length of utterances** (**MLU**). The MLU are the number of **morphemes** found in a sample of a child's utterances. A morpheme is the smallest unit of meaning in a word. For example, the prefix *bi* means *two* and is considered to be a morpheme. Thus, the word *bicycle* is made up of two morphemes—*bi* and *cycle*. The word *cat* is also a morpheme. There is some debate about what the MLU is for children of different ages. However, it is widely accepted that very young children produce MLUs which are shorter than older children. The MLU for a five-year-old is not going to be as long as that of a 10-year-old. For example, a five-year-old might say, "Do I have to go?" Whereas a 10-year-old might say, "Yeah, I know I was supposed to go five minutes ago." The expectations for speaking for children should be tailored to their development. Children should not be expected to produced utterances that are beyond their stage of development. For more information about child development see Chapter 1.

Pronunciation and young learners

As stated above, when young children are learning to speak in English as their native language, they sometimes have difficulty articulating specific phonemes such as /th/ or /r/. These difficulties can occur due to developmental factors. As most children grow and develop, they become able to **articulate** the different English-language phonemes. Some native-speaking children even need articulation therapy in order to learn how to pronounce certain sounds. Although I am a native speaker of English, I personally had trouble as a child with /r/ which was a bit embarrassing because I couldn't even pronounce my first name, Caroline, correctly. Fortunately, a speech therapist helped me learn how to properly articulate /r/.

Listed in Figure 2 are the sounds and ages when children should be expected to master different English-language sounds. It is not uncommon for children to learn many of these sounds at younger ages.

Age	Sounds Mastered
3 years	p, n, m, w, h, and all vowels
4 years	d, t, b, g, k, f
5 years	y, ing
6 years	l, j, sh, ch, wh
7 years	r, s, v
8 years	v, th, blends

Figure 2 Ages when native-English speakers usually master English-language sounds (Child Guidance Clinic)

Reflection

Make a list of 10 words that young children have difficulty pronouncing in your native language. How old are children who have trouble pronouncing these words? Does this difficulty continue as children develop? Are these English-language phonemes or do these phonemes exist in English? How could you incorporate special attention to these sounds in your lesson?

Share your answers with a classmate or colleague.

Overgeneralization of errors

Children have a tendency to **overgeneralize** grammar rules when they are learning English as their native language. Generalization is a vitally important aspect of human learning and involves inferring and deriving a rule, or law (Brown, 2000). One classic example of overgeneralization occurs with the use of the past tense. For example, *I seed the movie. I drawed the apple.*

Overgeneralization can also occur when a learner takes rules from his first language and applies them to a second or foreign language. For example, a Spanish-speaking child learning English might say, *I like ice cream chocolate*, instead of *I like chocolate ice cream.*

The process of learning one's native language, be it English or another language, requires a great deal of work. When teaching children to speak a second or foreign language, it is important to keep in mind the development of their skills in their native language. Time should be spent at home or at school helping children to develop skills in their native language because becoming proficient in any language requires attention to the process. ESL

or EFL instruction should not be at the expense of first-language development. Therefore, children should be given opportunities to develop skills in
their first language both at school and at home.

5. Classroom techniques and activities

Speaking activities are an important part of any young learners' ESL and
EFL classroom and are often considered the focal point of instruction. When
teaching speaking, it is especially important to select activities which match the
objectives of your program. For instance, if you teach in a school that emphasizes music and the arts, you would include a lot of songs authored by others
as well as by your students. The specific techniques and tasks that you choose
should be based on the aims of the program coupled with the learners' stages
of development.

Audiolingual Method (ALM)

The **Audiolingual Method (ALM)** to language teaching is based on
the notion that one can learn language by developing habits based on the
patterns of language (Celce-Murcia, 2001). There are two important features
of ALM which can easily be adapted for the young learner classroom: drills
with choral response and dialogues. The first feature typical of ALM is drills
aimed at getting learners to practice using the patterns that occur in language.
Substitution drills, such as in Example 2, are a hallmark of the ALM classroom. Note that one word is *substituted* in each line of the drill. Drill 1 below
would be appropriate for young learners at early stages of English-language
development as well as for young learners under the age of eight. Drill 2 is
what many consider to be more typical of ALM and would work especially
well with children who have studied English for some time or who are over
the age of eight. Older learners are better able to understand the concept of
adjectives and can make the substitution almost instantaneously when the
exercise is introduced. Younger children will need to do Drill 1 several times
and then later can move on to Drill 2.

Example 2

Substitution Drills

Drill 1

Children listen and repeat the sentences spoken by the teacher.

Teacher: *This is a yellow dress.*

Students: *This is a yellow dress.*

Teacher: *This is a blue dress.*

Drill 2

Students: *This is a blue dress.*

Teacher: *This is a red dress.*

Students: *This is a red dress.*

Teacher: *This is a yellow dress.*

Students: *This is a yellow dress.*

Teacher: *blue*

Students: *This is a blue dress.*

Teacher: *red*

Students: *This is a red dress.*

Teacher: *jacket*

Students: *This is a red jacket.*

Etc.

Although drills can be dull and boring for the learners, they do not have to be. Whenever possible, try to personalize the content to the learners in your classroom. For instance, do the drills in Example 2 based on the different clothes that some of your learners are wearing. Have them stand up while you point to the dresses they are wearing and lead the drill.

You can use drills for several minutes as a way to introduce a new language pattern to children. For instance, bring in pictures of food items as you pretend to eat different things or hold up pictures of an apple and say, *I like apples*. Then have the students repeat your sentence. You can also say each sentence and have students respond in unison, using the technique known as **choral response**.

Choral response is also used when children repeat the lines of a poem or song. Sentences with substitutions can be slipped right into the young-learner curriculum in the form of songs, chants, and finger-plays. When children are singing songs or finger-plays that have repetitive language and language substitutions, they are learning the patterns of the English language. Looking back at The Hokey-Pokey (page 48), you can easily see how the language resembles a substitution drill. When children sing the song, they are repeating the lines over and over again, and they are substituting words throughout the various verses. They are also repeating lines with one or two words changed or substituted for other lines.

Look back at the Action box on page 49 where you rewrote a finger-play or a song. Make a note of the basic pattern and list the words that were substituted.

Share your answer with a classmate or colleague.

Dialogues

The second feature of ALM which can easily find its way into the young learners' classroom is dialogue. Dialogues provide learners with grammatically controlled scripts that they can use in real life. Dialogues can very easily be scripted and turned into child-friendly role-plays. Whenever possible, the role-play should be based on the types of real and make-believe conversations that children have when they work and play.

Using puppets to introduce dialogues

Puppets can easily model different dialogues for children to practice with their classmates. You can also use puppets to show children how to work with a partner or in small groups. Teachers working with young learners are often aware that children feel more comfortable talking with a puppet than with an adult (Slattery and Willis, 2003). The use of puppets is very appropriate in the young-learner classroom. A child who developmentally is too shy to speak to an adult in front of his peers, may feel very comfortable when the same adult is holding a puppet and speaking to the child as the puppet. Puppets also make the language-learning activity more fun!

Fishbowl technique

One specific technique which helps children learn how to work with a partner or in a small group is known as the **fishbowl.** The teacher can either invite a volunteer to do the activity with him or can model the activity using two or more puppets. The teacher models the activity that the children are expected to do while everyone in the class watches as if the teacher and the volunteer were in a fishbowl. Children then go back to their seats knowing clearly what they are expected to do.

Example 3

Gogo Loves English 2 (Methold, Procter, Graham, McIntosh, Fitzgerald, 2001, pg. 39)

Using the textbook page in Example 3, the teacher has all of the children hold their coursebooks open to page 39 while she models how to do the page as a pair-work activity. As with all extracts in this book, T is for *teacher* and S is for *student*.

Extract 1

T: Where are the presents?

S: They're on the table.

T: Where's the umbrella?

S: It's under the table.

Communicative Language Teaching (CLT)

Teachers have realized the value of connecting real-life situations with classroom instruction and thus have embraced **Communicative Language Teaching. CLT** is an approach and a philosophical orientation that connects classroom-based language learning with the language that learners need in order to communicate outside of the classroom (Nunan, 2003). From the standpoint of teaching English to young learners, it is necessary to connect classroom learning to the real-life child-focused situations where children use language. There are many different situations where children use language to communicate and convey meaning such as asking a parent for help finding something that is lost, playing a game, saying a finger-play, inviting a friend over to play, and creating an art project.

CLT with children is slightly different than CLT with adults in part because children often enjoy playing the role of an adult or grown-up. They may, for example, find role-playing a flight attendant and an airline passenger to be an authentic activity even though in the real world they will not be, at least in the short term, a flight attendant. The activity can be authentic because it represents the type of authentic play, outside the classroom, that a young learner might engage in depending upon her interests and stage of development. This type of play is very meaningful for young learners in part because it gives them a chance to rehearse different language that they will use later on in life. For example, you may have played *teacher* as a child.

It is necessary to consider the type of language that children need in order to communicate in specific situations. For instance, if children are going to role-play finding a pair of lost socks, they would need to know the interrogative *where*. They might also need to know prepositions such as *in, on, under*, etc. Another instance would be when children are playing board games. They will need to be able say *first, next, last* as in spaces on the game and whose turn it is to play. If children are talking about a birthday party they had or went to, they will need to know the past tense.

In CLT, the focus is on getting the message across and helping children acquire **fluency.** In some cases, the language will need to be adjusted to meet the language level of the young learner. In other cases, the communicative task will require language that the children have not yet learned. When the task requires language that is unfamiliar to the children, I either modify the task or teach the necessary language. If I am teaching children a traditional game with a lot of steps, I may leave out some of the steps. For instance, if we are playing the game Concentration, I may omit the step that the child who gets a matching pair also gets an extra turn.

Make a list of two specific situations where 5- and 10-year-old children use language at home. Write down the vocabulary items and sentence patterns that children use for each situation. Think about how you could use the vocabulary and sentence patterns as a basis for a language activity.

Share your ideas with a classmate or colleague.

Games

Play is a purposeful activity and games are a part of playing. As such, games are a very appropriate teaching technique in the young-learner classroom. When carefully planned, games offer the advantages of both ALM and CLT. You can very easily set up games so that children repeat the same patterns over and over again. Games can also be structured to maximize English-language use. When I give the rules for a game, I always make using English a game rule. When English-use is a game rule, children tend to monitor their use of the English language while they play the game. For instance, if a child uses her native language while playing the game, she loses a point or a turn. There are a number of vocabulary games found in Chapter 6 (pages 128–132) which may also help children develop speaking skills.

One of my favorite games is Concentration, also known as Memory. This is a game which can be played with partners or in small groups. The game is made with two sets of 10 matching cards with vocabulary items that children are studying. The 20 cards are placed face down on a table. Each of the players says sentences prompted by the cards that they turn over. If the cards are the same, the player gets to "keep" them until the end of the game. If the cards are different, then the child places them face down in the same spot they originally found them. The winner is the player with the most cards at the end of the game.

Look at Extract 2. Two children are playing Concentration. Notice how the language patterns can serve as the basis for substitutions. Children are provided with a sentence pattern and then vary it as they see fit.

Extract 2

S1: (Turns over a picture of a chocolate candy bar.) *I like chocolate.*
(Turns over a picture of potatoes.) *I don't like potatoes.*

S2: (Turns over a picture of potatoes.) *I like potatoes.*
(Turns over a picture of apples.) *I like apples.*

S1: (Turns over a picture of potatoes.) *I don't like potatoes.*
(Turns over a picture of potatoes.) *I don't like potatoes.*

What are other games that would lend themselves to the language-learning classroom? Think about games that can be played with partners, in small groups, and in large groups.

Talking and Writing Box

In Chapter 1, I introduced the concept of the Talking and Writing Box (p. 11) as a way to learn about children's development and interests. The Talking and Writing Box is made of pictures that children have self-selected and are interesting to them. When children are asked to talk about the pictures on their box, they talk about things that are of interest to them because they have selected the pictures for the box.

I choose a topic each day. Then I have my students tell their talking partner their answer. I usually select two or three volunteers to talk about their answers. By using the Talking and Writing Box, children are able to personalize the information that they share. As you can see from Extract 3,

Children like to discuss their pets and families.

when talking about their pictures, children become animated because they are talking about something of interest to them.

> ### Extract 3
>
> **T:** *Which item on your box makes you smile?*
> **S:** *This picture.*
> **T:** *Why?*
> **S:** *It's my Uncle Donald. He is funny. On my birthday ...*

Figure 3 lists topics that children can talk about by looking at the pictures (or in) their Talking and Writing Box.

Which item is the biggest? Describe it.	Which item is the smallest? Describe it.	Which item is the biggest? Which item is the smallest? Compare the two.	Which item is the most colorful? Describe it.	Which item is the softest? Describe it.
Which item on your box has a nice smell?	Which item on your box is the prettiest to look at?	Which item on your box is the ugliest?	Describe three items on your box.	List four or five pictures of items which are found inside.
Which item on your box has a nice taste? Or, which item on your box would make you sick if you ate it?	Which item makes you smile? Why?	Which item on your box would you like to see come alive? Why?	Which item is the coldest? Describe the object and how to make it warm.	Which item is the hottest? Describe the object and how to make it cold.
Which item on your box would be the easiest to lose or misplace? Why?	If you were to give your box to someone special, who would you give it to?	Where did you get the pictures for your box?	Which item on your box will last a long time?	What would you like to store or keep in your box?
Which item feels the nicest when you touch it?	Which item feels funny when you touch it?	Which item would make a funny sound?	Which item wouldn't make any sound at all?	Which item could make a loud noise?

Figure 3 Talking and Writing Box topics

Teaching pronunciation

Rhymes, finger-plays, and chants help native English-speaking children learn how to pronounce words correctly. You can select rhymes and finger-plays that focus on a specific phoneme or sound or set of sounds. Most English-language coursebooks contain rhymes, poems, and chants as part of the program.

Children may have trouble pronouncing certain English-language sounds. For example, children who speak some Asian languages may have difficulty pronouncing the English-language /r/ and /l/ because of the way that they occur or their absences in their native languages. A speech therapist introduced me to the use of mirrors in the young-learner classroom. She pointed out that children who have difficulty with certain sounds often do not know how to form their lips and mouths in such a way as to correctly articulate the sounds. I was a little bit dubious at first as to whether the use of mirrors would help children improve their pronunciation but was amazed to see how well they worked. My sense is that the mirrors probably work so well because they give children an awareness of how easily they can adjust their pronunciation.

Tongue twisters are a fun way to teach pronunciation to children learning English as a second or foreign language. Tongue twisters generally have the same phoneme repeated over and over again. It is hard to articulate the same sound over and over again; thus the name tongue twister. Two of the most famous and popular tongue twisters are *Sally sells seashells at the seashore* and *Peter Piper picked a peck of pickled peppers. If Peter Piper picked a peck of pickled peppers, where's the peck of pickled peppers that Peter Piper picked? (or) how many peppers did Peter Piper pick?* Children adore tongue twisters because they perceive saying the sounds as a game or challenge. There are numerous tongue twisters available on the Internet. See Helpful Web Sites at the end of this chapter for a few suggestions. You may also create your own following the procedure found in the Action box below. In order to help children develop fluency, be sure to ask them if each tongue twister is a real sentence.

Action

1. Choose a letter of the alphabet and make a list of 10–20 words that begin with that letter. Be sure to include nouns, verbs, and adjectives. If you can't, come up with 10–15 words that start with that letter then choose another letter.

2. Make up a tongue twister with words from the list that have the same beginning sound. For example, *Cats cut cards*.

3. Think about how you would show young learners the meanings of the individual words.

Share your tongue twisters with a classmate or colleague.

Error correction

As caregivers, teachers of young learners must spend time correcting not only behavior but also errors. If you as a teacher of young learners correct every single error that children make, you would be utterly exhausted at the end of the day. Bailey (2005) points out that it is not necessary for a teacher to respond to all errors. I agree and don't respond to all the errors in my classroom. I think that responding to too many errors can discourage children from communicating and talking. I am also very cautious in how I respond to errors since I know that embarrassment and shame are two of the things that can be potentially damaging to young learners.

I like to handle errors by modeling and providing children with the correct grammar or pronunciation. I decide which errors I will focus on. I think about the children's development and any errors they may make because of interference from their native language. I also want to encourage fluency and try to make sure that I don't dampen the children's enthusiasm for communicating in English. Notice how in Extract 4 the teacher corrects errors.

Extract 4

T: *What does she do at 6:00?*

S1: *She do her math homework at 6:00.*

T: *She* does *her math homework at 6:00. Yes, she does her math homework at 6:00.* (Emphasizes the word *does*.) *Let's look at another picture. Tommy, what does he do at 7:00?*

S2: *He do karate.*

T: *He* does *karate. Yes, he* does *karate.* (The teacher pulls out the dog puppet, Winston.) *Winston, can you help us with something?*

W: (Teacher changes her voice to assume the role of Winston.) *Yes, I like to help.*

T: (Points to the third picture.) *Winston, what does he do at 6:00?*

W: *He* does *his English homework.*

T: *Good, Winston. All right everyone, what does he do at 6:00?*

Ss: *He does his English homework.*

T: *Very good. Again.*

Ss: *He does his English homework.* (The teacher continues the same procedure with other items.)

In Extract 4, the teacher notices the error and then models the correct response rather than telling the children that they were wrong. As soon as she notices that more than one child is making the same error, she stops and re-teaches the grammatical construction of the third person singular using the puppet. This way the error has been corrected and re-modeled without embarrassing any of the learners. The teacher then asks the children to respond. The teacher is very careful not to embarrass any of the children but rather just provide a model that the children can copy.

Think about how language errors were corrected when you were learning a foreign language. Were errors corrected in a subtle way as described above, or was an overemphasis placed on errors? How did you feel?

Share your answers with a colleague or classmate.

6. Managing speaking activities

When looking at language teaching, it is important to consider the technical knowledge of how people learn language with the practical, implicit, and intuitive knowledge that is gained through actual experience (Ellis, 1997). Nowhere is this basic concept truer than in managing speaking tasks with young children. For the pure sake of survival, it is crucial that you have well-planned lessons in order to maintain a certain level of control in your classroom. Well-planned lessons contain activities where children are interested and stay on task. Echevarria, Short, and Vogt (2000) emphasize the importance of lessons where children are at least 90 percent engaged and are appropriately paced.

Managing the noise level

During a speaking activity, the noise level alone can quickly escalate and disturb other classes. Teachers who do not use communicative approaches in their classrooms can be especially harsh if the noise level seems to become too high. As part of a well-rounded English-language curriculum, children should be given numerous opportunities to speak in class even though children can get loud, literally in a matter of seconds. Children can be taught a number of signals to become quiet. Do *not* try to shout over children. Think of how counter-productive it is for a teacher to shout, "ALL RIGHT EVERYONE! YOU ARE TOO NOISY!" when she herself is contributing to the noise level. Instead, it is much more productive to develop a visual cue to get children to be quiet and listen for the teacher's instructions. If the room is dark when the lights are turned off, the lights can be used as a signal. Another signal is for the teacher to raise one or both hands as a sign for children to stop what they are doing, including talking, raise their own hands, and wait for the teacher to give the next instruction.

Children can unwittingly drift into their mother tongue and not even realize that they have stopped using the target language. This is especially true if they have become very excited and engaged in the activity. It helps if they know exactly what they are supposed to do so that they don't need to ask for clarification of instructions. You can use the fishbowl technique described on page 54 above to show exactly what to do. I also like to give one instruction and wait to observe that everyone is on task and then give the next instruction.

7. Speaking in the classroom

In addition to games, children's coursebooks often help children practice specific language patterns and pre-scripted conversations. Sometimes it is hard to find activities that only focus on speaking since so many of the pages also contain print which adds reading to the activity. However, many of the exercises, such as Example 4 (page 64), are set up for children to do in pairs with a partner. Young learners take turns asking and answering questions as is seen in Extract 5 (page 64).

Example 4

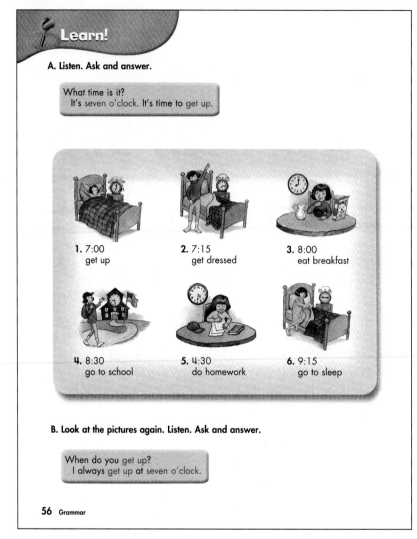

A. Listen. Ask and answer.

> What time is it?
> It's seven o'clock. It's time to get up.

1. 7:00
get up

2. 7:15
get dressed

3. 8:00
eat breakfast

4. 8:30
go to school

5. 4:30
do homework

6. 9:15
go to sleep

B. Look at the pictures again. Listen. Ask and answer.

> When do you get up?
> I always get up at seven o'clock.

56 Grammar

Hip Hip Hooray! 3 (Eisele, Hanlon, Eisele, Hanlon, Hojel, 2004, p. 56)

Extract 5

S1: *What time is it?*

S2: *It's seven o'clock. It's time to get up.*

S2: *What time is it?*

S1: *It's seven-fifteen. It's time to get dressed.*

After children are familiar with the pattern found in their book, they can personalize the content by using a toy clock as they talk about their own lives.

S1: *What time is it?*

S2: *It's four o'clock. It's time for soccer practice.*

Many coursebooks and teacher resource books contain pictures which can be legally photocopied, cut out, and mounted on heavy weight paper to create picture cards. Some of the picture cards are designed to help students practice a specific aspect of grammar. For instance, the pictures in Example 5 are from a teacher resource book and can be used to practice the present continuous by asking the question, "What's happening?"

Example 5

What's happening? PRIMARY GRAMMAR BOX 1.13

Picture cards

Baseboard

1	2	3	4
5	6	7	8

From *Primary Grammar Box* by C. Nixon and M. Tomlinson © Cambridge University Press 2003 *PHOTOCOPIABLE* 39

Primary Grammar Box: Grammar games and activities for younger learners (Nixon and Tomlinson, 2003, pg. 39)

Action

1. Look at the pictures in Example 5. Practice asking and answering each question. For example, "What's happening?" "He's drinking juice." "What's happening?" "The mouse is eating cheese." Continue with the other pictures.

2. You can also use the same set of pictures to practice different verb forms. Create a set of questions that you could use to practice a different verb form.

Share your answers with a classmate or colleague.

8. Conclusion

In this chapter, I discussed some of the issues that impact children learning to speak in English as their native language as well as English as a second or foreign language. I discussed ways of blending techniques designed primarily for children learning English as their primary language with approaches aimed at second- and foreign-language learners. Techniques for gently and kindly correcting children's errors were also presented. Finally, some of the challenges of and strategies for managing speaking tasks in a classroom with young learners were also presented.

Further readings

Conn-Beall, P., S. Hagen-Nipp, N. Spense-Klein, and L. Guida. 2002. *Wee Sing 25th Anniversary Celebration.* Los Angeles, CA: Price Stern Sloan.

This book and accompanying audio program are part of the Wee Sing series and provide a wealth of children's songs, chants, and finger-plays. The Wee Sing series has been used to teach millions of children favorite traditional and contemporary verse.

Graham, C. 1979. *Jazz Chants for Children.* New York, NY: Oxford University Press.

This classic part of the Jazz Chants series provides numerous child-centered chants which can fit into virtually any young-learner program.

Helpful Web sites

Songs for Teaching (www.songsforteaching.com)

This Web site provides a wealth of songs for teaching virtually every curriculum area.

There are also songs designed to help children who are learning English as a second language. There are chants and finger-plays which can be used for making transitions from one activity to another activity.

Tongue Twisters for Children
(www.indianchild.com/tongue_twisters.htm)

This site provides traditional and contemporary tongue twisters which are appealing to children of all ages.

References

Bailey, K. 2005. *Practical English Language Teaching: Speaking.* New York, NY: McGraw-Hill.

Birdsong, D. 1999. *Second Language Acquisition and the Critical Period Hypothesis.* Mahwah, NJ: Lawrence Erlbaum Associates.

Brown, H.D. 2000. *Principles of Second Language Learning and Teaching. 4th ed.* White Plains, NY: Addison Wesley-Longman.

Celce-Murcia, M. 2001. *Teaching English as a Second or Foreign Language. 3rd ed.* Boston, MA: Heinle & Heinle.

Child Guidance Clinic. *Child Guidance Clinic* [updated February 2005, cited 14 May 2005]. Available from http://www.childguidanceclinic.ca/.

Cook, G. 2000. *Language Play, Language Learning.* Oxford, UK: Oxford University Press.

Echevarria, J., D. Short, and M.E. Vogt. 2000. *Making Content Comprehensible for English Language Learners.* Needham, MA: Allyn & Bacon.

Eisele, B., R. Hanlon, C. Eisele, S. Hanlon, and B. Hojel. 2004. *Hip Hip Hooray! 3.* White Plains, NY: Longman Pearson Education.

Ellis, R. 1997. *SLA Research and Language Teaching.* Oxford, UK: Oxford University Press.

Marinova-Todd, S.K., B. Marshall, and C. Snow. 2003. Three Misconceptions about Age and L2 Learning. *TESOL Quarterly.* 34(1): 15–33.

Methold, K., S. Procter, M. Graham, M. McIntosh, and P. FitzGerald. 2001. *Gogo Loves English 2.* Hong Kong, PRC: Longman Asia ELT.

Nixon, C., M. Tomlinson. 2003. *Primary Grammar Box: Grammar games and activities for young learners.* Cambridge, UK: Cambridge University Press.

Nunan, D. 2003. Methodology. In D. Nunan (ed.), *Practical English Language Teaching.* New York, NY: McGraw-Hill, 3–22.

Slattery, M., and J. Willis. 2003. *English for Primary Teachers: Resource Book for Teachers of Young Students.* Oxford, UK: Oxford University Press.

Chapter **Four**

Teaching reading to young learners

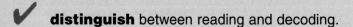

At the end of this chapter, you should be able to:

Goals

✔ **describe** the purposes and aims of reading.

✔ **distinguish** between reading and decoding.

✔ **describe** effective and ineffective phonics instruction.

✔ **explain** the advantages and disadvantages of using different approaches to reading.

✔ **demonstrate** familiarity with all of the techniques discussed in this chapter.

1. Introduction

The purpose of this chapter is to discuss reading as it pertains to children learning **ESL** or **EFL**. The chapter begins with a description of reading as it relates to children who are at different stages of literacy development in their native language. Basic background information about teaching reading is also provided. The next section is about developing reading skills and provides a discussion of phonics and literature-based approaches. Finally, information about a variety of strategies and techniques is presented including specific suggestions for using different textbook pages to teach different literacy skills.

2. What is reading?

Few of us can remember the exact moment when we learned how to read. This is mostly because we learned to read when we were very young and it is difficult to remember our very early years. Few of us can remember the moment when we suddenly knew that print represented meaning.

Reading is a set of skills that involves making sense and deriving meaning from the printed word. In order to read, we must be able to **decode** (sound out) the printed words and also comprehend what we read. For second-language learners there are three different elements which impact reading: the child's background knowledge, the child's linguistic knowledge of the target language, and the strategies or techniques the child uses to tackle the text (Peregoy and Boyle, 2004). For example, if a child is going to learn how to decode letters, she must understand what different written symbols represent. In some languages such as English, Spanish, Arabic, and Korean, a certain symbol represents a specific letter. These languages are known as **alphabetic languages**. For example, in Korean ㅑ represents the sound /ya/. However, in other languages, a certain symbol represents an entire word. For example, in Chinese the character 媽 represents the word *mother*. Furthermore, children who are able to read in their native language are at an advantage over children who cannot read in their native language because they understand the key concept that printed symbols can be used to represent spoken words. Also, children who can read in their native language may also know that reading can be for both pleasure and information. By developing strong literacy skills in their native language, it will be easier for young learners to transfer those skills into English.

Diaz-Rico and Weed (in-press) have identified concepts and skills that transfer from first-language literacy to second-language literacy (see Figure 1, page 70). Note that some of the concepts related to print such as directionality and letter names will depend upon the learner's native language because, as

Concepts and skills shown to transfer from first-language literacy to second-language literacy

- Print has meaning
- Reading and writing are used for various purposes
- Concepts about print
  - Book-orientation concepts (how to hold, to turn pages)
  - Directionality (left to right, top to bottom)
  - Letters (letter names, lower case, upper case)
  - Words (composed of letters, spaces mark boundaries)
- Knowledge of text structure
- Use of semantic and syntactic knowledge
- Use of cues to predict meaning
- Reading strategies (hypothesizing, constructing meaning, etc.)
- Confidence in self as reader

Figure 1 Concepts and skills that transfer from the first language to the second language (Diaz-Rico and Weed, in-press)

noted above, children whose first language uses characters will have more challenges than children whose first language uses letters to represent sounds.

However, even though there are differences between the development of literacy skills for languages with alphabetic writing systems and languages with other writing systems, there are many similarities including experimentation (Peregoy and Boyle, 2004). As a teacher of young learners, it is helpful to ascertain what reading concepts children have acquired in their native language so you can assist in the transfer of the relevant skills from first-language to second-language literacy.

Decoding

In order to read, we must recognize the symbols that form or make up words. When readers decode, they decipher individual words. Many languages use a phonetic alphabet. In these languages, written symbols represent a specific sound or phoneme. English has approximately 40 sounds but uses only 26 symbols (Moats, 2001). This can cause problems for speakers of languages which have a one-to-one sound-letter correspondence, such as Russian or Spanish. Because of the exceptions to sound/symbol correspondence in English, children can get very frustrated when they try to decode English words. For example, the letter *c* is used to decode both a hard and soft sound in English. The hard *c* sound, /k/, found in **c**at and **c**arpet is more common than the soft *c* sound, /s/, found in **c**ereal. However in Russian, the symbol *c* is always used to denote the soft /s/ sound.

Comprehension

The aim of reading is comprehension (Anderson, 2003). Some individuals equate decoding with reading. Just because a learner knows how to pronounce written words correctly, doesn't mean that he can read.

1. Try to find a text written using a writing system you know, but in a language you don't know. For example, if you speak Spanish, find a text written in French or Italian.

2. Pronounce the words of the text. Although you will have some success decoding the words, you will not have understood the text.

3. Unfortunately, teachers often assume that students who can read aloud are comprehending what they are reading. In the classroom, what are three strategies you could use to check if students are just decoding or are decoding and comprehending what they are reading?

Share your strategies with a classmate or colleague.

3. Background to the teaching of reading

Reading comprehension refers to reading for meaning, understanding, and entertainment. It involves higher-order thinking skills and is much more complex than merely decoding specific words. Teaching children how to derive meaning as well as analyze and synthesize what they have read is an essential part of the reading process. Here are two main reasons that people read: the first is for pleasure and the second is for information.

This little girl has learned that books can bring us pleasure.

What was one of your favorite books as a child? Was it fiction or non-fiction? Why did you like it? What is one of your favorite books today? Is it fiction or non-fiction? Why do you like it? Did these books provide information or entertainment or a combination of both?

Share your answers with a classmate or colleague.

Reading for pleasure

Think about how much fun it is to read or listen to a good story. Stories provide enjoyment for readers of all ages. Literature belongs in every class-room for young learners, whether the learners are native speakers or non-native speakers of English. It is surprising that until recently, modern English Language Teaching (ELT) coursebooks did not make more use of stories, a fundamental and enjoyable aspect of the target language (Hill, 2001). Fortunately, modern coursebooks are increasingly using stories as a vital component.

The children are enjoying a story with their mother.

Bedtime stories are wonderful because children see themselves as getting a double treat. Often they think that they get to stay up late *and* get to listen to a story. Children are unaware that when they listen to a story being read aloud, they are being introduced to the idea that reading can be used as a form of enter-tainment. As a teacher, encourage parents to read to their children as much as possible. Even if they are reading in the child's native language, the rewards will carry over into the child's English-language development. For example, if a student knows that she can get pleasure from reading stories in her own language, she may be able to make the connection that reading in general can provide pleasure.

When you were a child, what was your favorite story? Was it a story that was read to you or was it one that you read yourself? Who were the main characters? Was it real or a made-up story? What made it interesting?

Share your answers with a classmate or colleague.

Reading for information

Your purpose for reading this book is to get information. You may be a new teacher to the ELT profession or an experienced teacher wanting to learn more about the latest trends in teaching young learners. Regardless of your situation, you are reading to learn more about teaching English to young learners.

Reading for information can be as simple as reading a menu at a restaurant. If a young learner's mother uses a cookbook, the child may help by reading different parts of the recipe to her mother. A child interested in dinosaurs might enjoy reading a passage about the prehistoric animals. A child who wants to make a model airplane may be motivated to read a book about model airplanes or the instructions in a model airplane kit. Reading for information can also give children pleasure.

The girls are reading simple instructions so they can make something special.

1. Besides this book, what different pieces of non-fiction have you read in the last 24 hours? Did you read an article from a newspaper, magazine, or Web site? Did you read recipes or bus schedules? What did you read in English? What did you read in another language?

2. What are different pieces of non-fiction that young children would be interested in?

Share your list with a classmate or colleague.

Vision problems

When children with poor eyesight are learning to read in their native language, they can often decipher fuzzy or unclear symbols because they can draw upon their vast oral language knowledge to help determine specific patterns of symbols and words from context. However, it is much more difficult for these children to decipher unclear symbols in English.

Children who have any signs of vision problems should be tested to see if they need glasses. Children who wear glasses may need to have their vision prescriptions changed every few years. They may also need to be gently encouraged to wear their glasses. Usually children who are nearsighted–can only see things close-up–should sit close to the board. Figure 2 lists some of the behaviors that could indicate vision problems.

- Squints, closes/covers one eye
- Holds a book close to the face
- Holds a book far away from the face
- Strains and moves one's head to see the board
- Loses place while reading
- Complains of headaches after reading or doing close work
- Complains of double vision
- Tilts head to one side
- Is generally unaware that one eye wanders
- Has trouble reading from the board or copying from the board

Figure 2 Indicators of possible vision problems

Configurations

Often when teachers begin teaching decoding, they use block letters (all capital letters). However, when you look at words printed with lower case letters, it is easier to make out the shape of the word than when you look at a word printed entirely with block letters. This is known as the configuration or shape make up of the letters within a word. Look at the words in Figure 3. Note that although the word is the same, it is easier to make out the word written with the lower case letters than the word with the upper case letters. Pay careful attention to the way some parts of the words go above and others go below the line.

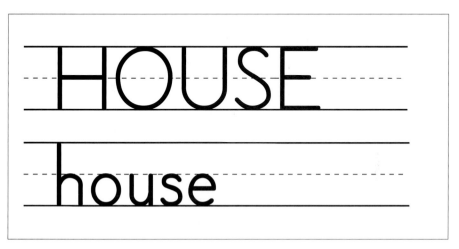

Figure 3 Block letters compared to lower case letters

Because the configuration of block letters is more difficult to read, it is better to be careful when you use them with young learners. If you are including authentic **environmental print** as part of your reading program, you will notice that some signs are printed with all capital letters such as the word *STOP*. However, generally speaking, you will want to avoid block letters.

4. The development of reading skills

If you were to visit a kindergarten class for native English speakers, you would undoubtedly see children engaged in a variety of activities. On the surface, some of these activities might look as if they are not very educational. However, activities such as doing art projects with patterns, listening to and talking about stories, playing with words, and learning the symbols that represent words, all help children in their quest to learn how to read. These activities are specifically designed to give children the knowledge of oral language, symbolic and pattern representation, and higher-order thinking skills they will need to both decode and comprehend written words.

Think about how you learned to read. Do you remember reading with your parents? What did your reading books look like? Did your parents help you with reading? Did you learn how to read at school? Was reading easy or difficult for you? What made it easy or difficult?

Share your answers with a classmate or colleague.

Often when native English-speaking children are taught to read, they are taught how to read for both pleasure and for information. This is reflected in many of the reading coursebooks. If you were to look at a coursebook for native English-speaking children, you would notice that there is a variety of fiction and non-fiction selections aimed at helping children learn that reading can be pleasurable and informative.

When native English speakers are taught how to read, there is a great deal of variation on the amount of emphasis placed on decoding and reading for comprehension. **Phonics** (sound-letter correspondence) and decoding does not lead a child to becoming a lifelong reader. As a teacher of young learners, you want to make sure that children perceive reading as a tool. Children need to be taught to see reading as a key that will open many different doors.

Phonics-based instruction

Phonics-based instruction is intended to teach students the basic English-language phonics rules so that they can easily decode words. Within English-language programs for native speakers as well as ESL and EFL programs, the amount of attention paid to phonics varies from none to a great deal. "The purpose of phonics instruction is to teach beginning readers that printed letters represent speech sounds heard in words" (Heilman, 2002, p. 1). Phonics instruction is intended to help children see the correspondence between letters and sounds. While decoding is one of the first stepping stones to reading, it's important to remember that decoding is different from reading.

Not only is there confusion between reading and phonics, there also can be confusion between pronunciation and phonics. Phonics is the teaching of sounds as part of decoding. Pronunciation, on the other hand, refers to the way one articulates specific sounds. This confusion is understandable because if you do not have good pronunciation, it can be more difficult to distinguish between different English-language phonemes. However, it's important to remember that pronunciation is only concerned with sounds, and phonics-based instruction is concerned with teaching children that letters can be put together to form words.

It is important to always keep meaning in focus when providing phonics instruction. It can be very easy to overemphasize phonics. One of the problems with phonics is that teachers and their young learners can become overly focused on decoding and not concerned enough with meaning.

Phonics instruction should be based on the English words that children already have in their oral-language repertoire. In addition, learners should already know how to pronounce the word before they are expected to sound it out or read it. They should not have to struggle with pronunciation and phonics simultaneously.

Phonics instruction must be carefully planned for children learning how to read in ESL and EFL classrooms. As mentioned in Chapter 2, too often the words used to represent different sounds are not commonly used by children. When children are at the **emergent literacy** stage, they should never be expected to read a word that they don't know the meaning of. For this reason, it's important to align your vocabulary and phonics instruction.

A caution about phonics instruction: I have seen an emphasis on phonics instruction that forces children to focus so much on the individual sounds that they don't recognize that they are reading words, sentences, stories, or pieces of non-fiction. Phonics instruction should enhance comprehension. It should not be allowed to detract from meaning-based instruction. As Peregoy and Boyle (2004, p. 61) reminds us, "English learners should not be involved in phonics instruction that isolates sounds and letters from meaningful use in text."

In order to help insure that the phonics portion of your program has the right emphasis, you may want to look at Figure 4. It lists some considerations you should take into account when implementing phonics into the reading portion of your English-language program.

Effective phonics instruction	Ineffective phonics instruction
• sustains a brisk pace • matches what is read with concepts and strategies being taught • engages children in activities that are relevant and purposeful • includes writing as a significant component • emphasizes chunks and patterns in words • differentiates lessons based on individual children's needs	• dominates literacy instruction for all children • emphasizes the memorization of rules • emphasizes words in isolation • bases lessons on worksheets • uses decodable texts as the primary resource in reading • takes up a lot of instructional time every day • places a heavy emphasis on phonics beyond what children need

Figure 4

(continued)

• engages children in decision-making and hands-on activities • exposes children to a variety of texts • integrates what is learned in a variety of authentic reading and writing texts	• requires children to master phonics before learning to read

Figure 4 Characteristics of effective and ineffective phonics instruction (Bergeron and Bradbury-Wolff, 2002, p. 61)

Literature-based approach

The literature-based approach is designed to help young learners develop literacy skills within the context of literature. Instruction utilizing literature is also based on the premise that literacy is an inter-related process (Popp, 1996). Currently, the value of picture books is continuing to be acknowledged in ESL and EFL programs.

Ellis and Brewster (2000) delineate over 25 reasons why authentic storybooks should be used in classrooms where children are learning English as a second or foreign language. Their multitude of reasons can be divided into two categories: the development of the child as an intellectual and creative being and the authentic English language and culture that is contained in children's storybooks. An underlying premise of the list is that stories can be enjoyed by young learners and can be used to help children develop a host of cognitive and social skills. Literature-based instruction is designed to help children develop an appreciation and enjoyment of literature while at the same time developing literacy skills.

One final note: while individuals often think of phonics-based instruction and the literature-based approach as being exclusive teaching tools, phonics-based instruction can easily be combined with a literature-based approach. By helping children focus on different aspects of print, you will help them begin to make an association between reading skills and reading for pleasure.

5. Classroom techniques and activities

There are many different reading and pre-reading activities that can help children develop reading skills in English. The activities that you choose should be based on the individual child's development, native-language literacy skills, and oral-language skills in English. As a teacher, you will also have to consider the aims or objectives of your school's English-language program. It is also important to remember that reading activities should be carefully sequenced to build upon one another.

Phonics

One of the easiest ways to begin phonics instruction is by introducing sounds and letters that are associated with specific nouns. Some teachers believe that children should be taught the letters and sounds of the alphabet in alphabetical order. However, other teachers, myself included, start children with the consonants that follow fairly regular spelling patterns including: /m/, /s/, /t/, /l/, /n/, and /r/.

When I introduce phonics in the classroom, I start by teaching the initial sounds and letters of words, usually nouns. For example, if you are teaching students the letter *m*, you would also teach them that *m* makes the /m/ sound. Look at Extract 1 from a class of seven- and eight-year-old children who have had one year of English instruction and are just beginning English-language literacy instruction. As with all extracts in this book, T stands for *teacher* and S stands for *student*.

Extract 1

T: *Today we are going to talk about what words start with the /m/ sound. What words start with the /m/ sound?* (The teacher writes the letter *M* on the board.)

S1: *Monkey.* (The teacher writes the word *monkey* on the board under the letter *M*.)

T: *Good. Monkey. Monkey starts with the /m/ sound. What letter makes the /m/ sound?*

Ss: *M*

T: *Very good. The letter M makes the /m/ sound. Can you give me the name of another word that starts with the /m/ sound?*

S2: *Mouse.* (The teacher writes the word *mouse* on the board.)

T: *Very good. Can you point to a picture of a mouse?* (Students point to a picture of a mouse on the wall.) *Good. Who can tell me another word that starts with the /m/ sound?*

S3: *Milk.* (The teacher writes *milk* on the board.)

T: *Very good. How about another word?*

S4: *Move.* (The teacher writes the word *move* on the board.)

T: *Good. Move starts with the /m/ sound. Can everyone move their head?* (Students move their heads.) *Good. Now I would like a volunteer to come and circle the letter M and make the same sound as the letter.*

Note that in Extract 1, all of the children called out words that did indeed start with the /m/ sound. The teacher wrote the words on the board under the letter *m*. If a child had given a word that didn't start with *m*, the teacher could write the word off to the side and not under the letter *m*. She could then go back to the *m* words that she had written and help the children figure out the initial letter and sound of the word.

Make a list of different words that start with the following consonant sounds /s/, /b/, /t/, /l/, and /n/. Be sure to include words that young learners are familiar with. Create a mini-lesson following the example in Extract 1.

Share your answers with a classmate or colleague.

There are many ways for young learners to learn the initial sounds of words. They can cut out pictures of words that start with different letters and then match the pictures with the letters. They could also sort pictures that start with a specific phoneme or sound. For example, they could make a collage with pictures of things that start with the letter *m* including pictures of a *man, moon, melon, monkey,* and *mask.*

Once children are familiar with the initial sounds made by different consonants, they are ready to start learning short vowel sounds. Often it is easier to start with the short *a* sound /ă/ than the other short vowel sounds. Children can be taught that /ă/ makes the short vowel sound as in *apple.*

When young learners know short vowel sounds and their initial and final consonant sounds, they are ready to learn how to blend sounds together. At this point in your instruction, you can introduce children to the concept of blending sounds by printing words on the board that follow a consonant-vowel-consonant (CVC) pattern. The words *bat, dog,* and *run* follow the CVC pattern. The CVC pattern is used because it is considered to be very predictable, and children will quickly experience success decoding words when they use it.

In addition, draw an arrow under the word going from left to right. Show children how to move their finger and blend the sounds to form the word.

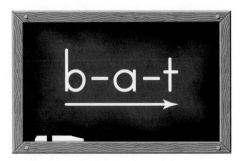

Point to each individual letter in the word and then ask students to identify the sound made by each letter. Move a pointer from left to right below each letter as you prompt students to sound out the word. Once students are able to sound out the word, ask a volunteer to come to the board and draw a picture of a bat. This will help to insure that the learners can comprehend the words that they are reading.

Predictable stories and pattern books

One type of story that is prominent in English-language programs is the predictable story. The predictable story contains repetitive phrases and predictable language. Predictable storybooks, also called pattern books, contain illustrations that help to clarify or support the word, sentence, or pattern that is repeated in the text (Optiz, 1995). Since pattern books contain the same words and phrases, children are exposed to the same words repeated over and over again.

Pattern books, such as *Mrs. Wishy-Washy* (Cowley, 1999), can be used to help children develop phonics skills as well as an appreciation for literature.

Example 1

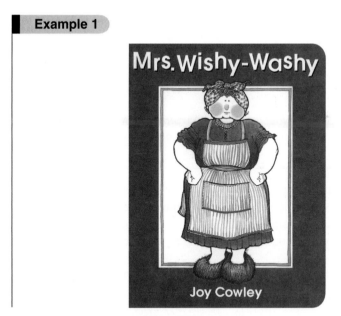

Mrs. Wishy-Washy (Cowley, 1999, cover)

In Extract 2, the teacher has just finished reading *Mrs. Wishy-Washy* to her six-year-old students. Notice how she draws their attention to the print found in the book.

> **Extract 2**
>
> **T:** *Let's look at the cover of the book again. Can you point to the letter W?* (Students point to the W.) *What sound does the letter W make?*
>
> **Ss:** /w/
>
> **T:** *Good. It makes the /w/ sound. Now let's look at the next letter. What letter is it?*
>
> **Ss:** I
>
> **T:** *Good. It is I. What sound does it make?*
>
> **Ss:** /i/
>
> **T:** *What sound do they make together?*
>
> **Ss:** /wi/
>
> **T:** *Now let's look at the next word. What sound does it make at the beginning?*
>
> **Ss:** /w/
>
> **T:** *Now let's look at the next letter. What sound does it make?*
>
> **Ss:** /a/
>
> **T:** *Good. Now look at these two words. What sound do they make in the beginning?*
>
> **Ss:** /w/
>
> **T:** *Good. Now look at both words. Look at the second letter. What is the difference between the beginnings of each word?*

Action

Find a children's pattern book in English. Create a phonics-based lesson using the cover of the book. If you do not have access to a children's book in English, create your own storybook. Many of the songs and finger-plays found in the appendix can be used as the basis of your book.

Share your answer with a classmate or colleague.

> **Postage for authentic English-language picture books**
>
> One challenge in countries where English is a foreign language can be obtaining authentic English-language books at affordable prices. Often, when you send books to yourself or have friends send books to you, the cost of postage is greater than the cost of the books themselves. However, every country I have taught in has had *M-bags* offered by the country's public post office. M-bags are designed to ship books and other printed matter from one place to another. M-bags are available from and to most countries. To obtain an M-bag, you need to go to the local post office and say that you want to ship books. I have found this service to be very reliable. For example, I have been able to ship books from the United States to Latvia and from Belarus to South Korea for very little money.

Sight words

Sight words are **high-frequency** words children can recognize on sight without having to decode the letters. *The, all, an,* and *I* are all sight words. Some sight words are especially difficult to sound out or decode because they do not follow regular spelling patterns–*right, there, look,* and *should.* Games are engaging ways to teach sight words. For example, young learners can go through a piece of text and count how many times the word *the* occurs in the text. You can also make a path-style board game with different sight words. Children throw a dice and move spaces. Whenever they land on the sight word, they read it aloud.

Names

Children's names can be sight words. Children enjoy reading their own names. An alternative way to call attendance is to print each child's name on a different card. You can then show the names while children read them aloud. This technique works well with young learners who use their own real names written with Latin letters (a, b, c, …) or when children use nicknames again written with English-language letters.

Print-rich environment

Hudelson (1994) points out that children who come from societies filled with print are likely to learn at a very early age that print serves different purposes or functions. Print-rich environments encourage and invite children to develop literacy skills (Collins, 2004). In English-language classrooms, print-rich environments contain English-language environmental print prevalent in countries where English is the main language of communication. Environmental print is the print that is seen all around us. It is the print on signs, labels, billboards, etc. Even in countries where English is not the primary medium of communication, there are often English-language signs, such as the names of hamburger outlets, pizza parlors, and gas stations. These establishments will often give authentic pieces of environmental print for free.

As a teacher, you should try to create a print-rich environment in the classroom. The print should have meaning for the learners. You should include as much environmental print as possible. Be sure to include items such as the following:

- bulletin boards with English-language labels such as *Our Work*
- labels such as *desk, door, window*
- word lists with vocabulary words that children are learning
- authentic literature, storybooks, and non-fiction titles in English
- posters with English-language labels, such as travel posters
- English-language packages, such as cereal box packages
- English-language calendars

One good place for a print-rich display is on your classroom door. One advantage of using the classroom door is that all of the children pass through the door when they come and go to class. Also, children might have to wait at the door before or after each lesson. Plus, you can use the print on the door as mini-lessons. You can also tape things to the windows and then use a razor blade to remove any evidence that the windows were used as make-shift bulletin boards. You can help children apply phonics rules with these different sight words. For example, if you are pointing at the word *door* on the door, you can ask, "What letter does this start with? What sound does the letter *d* make?"

Action

1. Make a list of all the environmental print that you have seen in the last 24 hours. It is not necessary for the print to have been in English. Think about the different types of signs found in different parts of your region or town. For example, have you seen subway signs or signs for stores and restaurants?

2. Circle the items that can be replicated in English and placed in your classroom.

3. With a classmate or colleague, discuss the following questions: which items on your list are topics frequently taught to young learners? Which items would be interesting to young learners?

Learning centers

Learning centers are stations or places within a classroom where children can work alone, in pairs, or in small groups. You can create learning centers with environmental print focused on specific topics. For example, you could create an airline travel learning center. The next time you are on a plane, you can pick up some English-language material from the flight. You could also use the material as part of a role-play about travel.

Language experience approach

The **language experience approach** is used to help native English-speaking, ESL, and EFL children develop beginning literacy skills. Please note that many may consider the language experience approach to be more of a technique than an approach; others such as Peregoy and Boyle (2005) view it as an approach. The language experience approach can be a meaningful and pleasurable group literacy experience. Learners participate in a group activity and then describe what happened in their own words. The teacher serves as a scribe and writes down everything that the children say on giant size paper. Some teachers write down the words exactly as the children say them. Other teachers, myself included, will make minor editorial corrections so that the grammar is correct. Children then read and re-read the text with their teacher. The teacher can also use the text for phonics instruction.

The group activity can be as simple as drinking juice or as complicated as going on a field trip. For example, after a visit to a local bakery, students may say and the teacher may write:

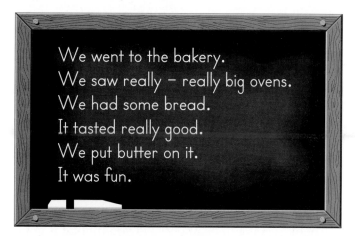

We went to the bakery.
We saw really – really big ovens.
We had some bread.
It tasted really good.
We put butter on it.
It was fun.

The language experience approach can also work with individual children. You can ask a child to describe what he did over the weekend. The child dictates the story to you or another learner with more advanced English-language literacy skills.

Own words

Sylvia Ashton-Warner (1985) taught English to Maori children in New Zealand and used a number of techniques including children's own words to help young learners acquire English literacy skills. Each morning when the students walked in, she would ask them what words they would like to learn and she would write down their words, in English, on small cards. The children would quickly learn the words because they had personal meaning. As a teacher, you can ask children to come up with their own words related to the topics they are currently studying or words they would just like to know. These words can be written on small index cards or in the students' notebooks. Find an opportunity each week to individually review the words with each child.

Reflection

1. Write down three or four words that are important to you today.

2. Now write down three or four words that were important to you when you were a child. Think about why these words were important.

3. If you were a young learner today, would you be likely to remember the words? Why or why not?

Share your answers with a classmate or colleague.

Questioning techniques

Since comprehension is the aim of reading, you should provide students with focused instruction on comprehending written texts. In this section, I have provided questions to check comprehension and several strategies that have helped my students to improve their comprehension. In Chapter 2, guidelines for listening comprehension questions were provided on page 37.

The judicious use of questions is very important. During a reading lesson, questions should be used to check comprehension and to help children think about what they are reading. Before children read, you should ask questions to pique their interest. For example, you might ask, "What do you think this book is going to be about? Do you think it is going to be scary? Why or why not? Have you ever been to a place like this?"

Watch the faces of your learners as you ask different questions. Make sure that the number and type of questions you ask does not detract from the enjoyment of reading. Your questions should generate interest and enthusiasm for what is being read. They should not make the children feel apprehensive about not answering correctly. Try to ask questions that help children become involved with the text. For example, if you are sharing the picture book *Testing Miss Malarkey* (Example 2) with 10- and 11-year-old students, you could ask the questions in Figure 5 to check comprehension and to get learners to use the context.

Example 2

Testing Miss Malarkey (Finchler and O'Malley, 2000. p. 17)

What do you see in the picture?

What is the boy's mother saying?

How can you tell what she is saying?

How do you think the boy feels?

How can you tell how he feels?

Do you think his mom should give him a worksheet or ditto as part of his bedtime story? Why or why not?

Figure 5 Possible comprehension questions for *Testing Miss Malarkey*

You can also use questions to help students become interested in a piece of non-fiction. For instance, if you are reading a book about trucks with five- or six-year-olds you could ask, "Which one do you like the best? Which one do you think is the biggest? Which one do you think would go the fastest? Why?"

Comprehension strategies

Many years ago when I started teaching children, I worked with another teacher whose students could sound out words very well but had trouble comprehending what they had read. She told me that the children could say words but could not read. This frustrated her a bit because her focus was on comprehension and not decoding. Her mantra to her young learners was, "Reading is hard work and understanding what you have read is the hardest part." She recognized the importance of teaching children strategies or techniques to help them focus on the meaning represented by the words. Below are a number of simple strategies that can help children improve their comprehension skills.

Context clues and print conventions

Learning how to use **context** is an invaluable tool in comprehension. Sometimes when I am teaching beginning readers, I cover the picture on the page I'm reading and ask my students to tell me what is under my hand. Often beginning readers are so focused on decoding that they do not even notice the pictures. Once children realize that they haven't paid attention to the pictures, they begin to discover pictures can give us clues regarding the content.

In addition to pictures, you can teach children print conventions that facilitate comprehension. For example, children should be taught that capital letters in English are used for proper names of people and places. Then if a child comes across a word in the middle of the sentence with a capital letter, he can assume that it is the name of a person or place.

Knowing how punctuation marks work can also facilitate reading. Children who are six years old can learn that when we read, we pause at a period because it is the end of a complete thought or that an exclamation point tells us that something with emotion has just occurred or that a question mark lets us know that a question is being asked. Seven-year-olds can begin to learn that a comma reminds us to have a little tiny pause before we continue reading.

Graphic organizers

Graphic organizers are tools to help learners visually organize the information that they have read or will read. A wide variety of graphic organizers can be used to help students tackle and comprehend challenging texts (Burke, 2000). Three of the most popular graphic organizers are KWL charts, semantic maps, and Venn diagrams.

KWLs (Example 3) are used for learners to organize information before and after they read a passage. The first two columns are done prior to reading the passage. *K* refers to what a learner already knows about the topic. *W* is for what the learner wants to learn. After learners have read the passage, they fill out the third column with what they have learned (*L*).

Example 3

What I **Know**	What I **Want to Know**	What I **Learned**
that dinosaurs lived many years ago	the reason that the dinosaurs died	no one really knows for sure why they died

Semantic maps are meaning maps where information is grouped into different clusters. There are a variety of ways to group the information. For instance, you can put information about each character into different bubbles. Example 4 is a semantic map about the characters of "Goldilocks and the Three Bears."

Example 4

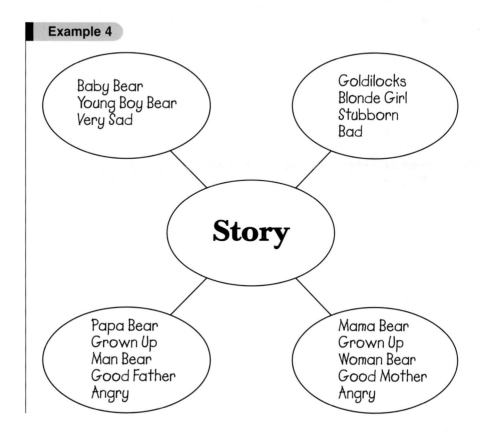

Choose a famous children's story and create a semantic map for the characters in the story.

Share your map with a classmate or colleague.

Venn diagrams are used to compare and contrast information. If, for example, children are reading about different animals, they can easily create a Venn diagram to show what they have learned. Example 5 shows a Venn diagram completed by a young learner after reading about a cow and a horse. The Venn diagram allows the learner to see the differences and similarities of the two animals.

Example 5

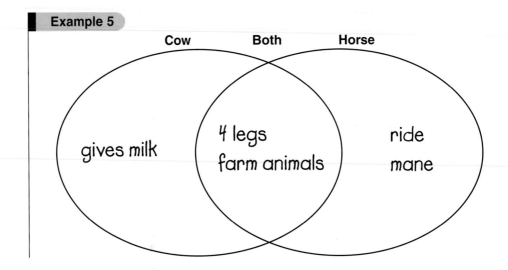

Cow   Both   Horse

gives milk

4 legs
farm animals

ride
mane

6. Reading in the classroom

Reading can easily be integrated into any program for teaching English to young learners. The amount of time you devote to reading and the development of reading skills will depend upon the goals of your program. How much time is spent developing literacy skills will also depend upon the coursebooks you are using with your learners. Regardless of the English-language reading objectives, it is important to remember to include reading for pleasure and reading for information.

A variety of strategies

Children can be taught a variety of reading strategies. Before you begin any reading lesson, or even mini-reading lesson, help children use context clues to determine meaning. When using coursebooks, be sure to direct children to look for the environmental print. For example, if you are looking at a scene page of the inside of a school, you might want to point out the picture of the library. You could ask children what is inside the library. You may want to also help children use phonics skills to decode the specific word, such as the sign "Library." At the very least, direct students to pay attention to the word *library* in their books. Encourage children to look at the context and figure out what the different signs say. Example 6 is a book designed for four- to six-year-old young learners.

Example 6

Bubbles 3 (Kleinert, 2004, p. 42 and 43)

Action

Using the page from Example 6, create an extract between a teacher and the students. The focus should be on helping the students learn the meanings of the different signs in the picture.

Share your answers with a classmate or colleague.

Young learners should also be taught comprehension strategies when they read pieces of text for information. Children often enjoy reading short magazine-style articles in their ESL or EFL coursebooks. Students can be taught strategies for comprehending informational texts. Example 7 is a book intended for eight- to 10-year-old children who have some English-language literacy skills.

Example 7

Best Friends 3 (Sileci, 2002, p. 86)

Action

Create two different graphic organizers for the coursebook page in Example 7.

Share your graphic organizers with a classmate or colleague.

Engage learners

One of the things that is so nice about children's picture books is that the pictures are often very engaging. It is important to draw children's attention to interesting and imaginative illustrations as a way to make reading a pleasurable experience. Carefully worded questions can help children become interested in the story.

Example 8

Not Now, Bernard (McKee, 1980, cover)

Action

Look at the cover of *Not Now, Bernard* (Example 8, page 93). Come up with a list of questions that would prompt children to be interested in the story.

Share your answers with a classmate or colleague.

7. Conclusion

In this chapter, decoding and comprehension were presented as they relate to reading and reading instruction. The two main purposes of reading were discussed—reading for pleasure and reading for information. The chapter also provided a background to the teaching of reading which included the distinction between decoding and reading. The use of authentic materials including environmental print as well as materials which are intended for ESL and EFL learners were also discussed. Information on how to use a variety of techniques to teach reading were provided.

Further readings

Bergeron, B.S. and M. Bradbury-Wolff. 2002. *Teaching Reading Strategies in the Primary Grades.* New York, NY: Scholastic Books.

This book presents a host of very practical suggestions for teaching a variety of reading strategies. Emphasis is placed on developing comprehension-based strategies. A number of useful reproducible pages are provided.

Heilman, A.W. 2002. *Phonics in Proper Perspective.* 9th ed. Upper Saddle River, NJ: Merrill-Prentice Hall.

This is an invaluable little book if you wish to include phonics-based instruction as part of your English-language program. It combines theory with practice.

Helpful Web sites

The International Children's Digital Library (www.icdlbooks.org)

This site provides on-line free access to published children's book. This project has been funded by the National Science Foundation and the Institute for Museum and Library Sciences and is striving to create a collection of over 10,000 books in 100 languages.

The International Reading Association (IRA) (www.reading.org)

The International Reading Association (IRA) is a professional organization dedicated to the improvement of reading for school-age learners around the world. A discounted membership price is offered to teachers in countries which have been designated as developing.

References

Anderson, N. 2003. Reading. In D. Nunan (ed.), *Practical English Language Teaching*. New York, NY: McGraw-Hill, 67–86.

Ashton-Warner, S. 1985. *Teacher*. New York, NY: Touchstone Books: Simon and Schuster.

Bergeron, B.S. and M. Bradbury-Wolff. 2002. *Teaching Reading Strategies in the Primary Grades*. New York, NY: Scholastic Books.

Burke, J. 2000. *Reading Reminders: Tools, Tips and Techniques*. Portsmouth, NH: Heinemann Boynton/Cook.

Cameron, L. 2001. *Teaching Languages to Young Learners*. Cambridge, UK: Cambridge University Press.

Collins, K. 2004. *Growing Readers*. Portland, ME: Stenhouse Publishers.

Cowley, J. 1999. *Mrs. Wishy-Washy*. Bothel, WA: The Wright Group.

Cunningham, A. and R. Shagoury. 2005. *Starting with Comprehension: Reading Strategies for the Youngest Learners*. Portland, ME: Stenhouse Publishers.

Diaz-Rico, L. and K. Weed. In Press. *The Crosscultural, Language and Academic Development Handbook: A Complete K-12 Reference Guide*. Boston, MA: Allyn and Bacon.

Ellis, G. and J. Brewster. 2002. *Tell It Again: The New Storytelling Handbook for Primary Teachers*. London, UK: Longman, Penguin Books.

Finchler, J. and K. O'Malley. 2000. *Testing Miss Malarkey*. New York, NY: Walker & Company.

Gunning, T.G. 2004. *Creating Literacy Instruction for All Children*. Boston, MA: Allyn and Bacon.

Heilman, A.W. 2002. *Phonics in Proper Perspective. 9th ed*. Upper Saddle River, NJ: Merrill-Prentice Hall.

Hill, D. 2003, Survey: Graded Readers. *ELT Journal*, 55(3): 300–24.

Hudelson, S. 1994. *Literacy Development of Second Language Children* (Gennese, F., ed) *Educating Second Language Children: The whole child, the whole curriculum, the whole community*. Cambridge, UK: Cambridge University Press.

Kleinert, G. 2004. *Bubbles 3*. New York, NY: McGraw-Hill ELT.

Optiz, M. 1995. *Getting the Most from Predictable Books: Strategies and Activities for Teaching with More than 75 Children's Books.* New York, NY: Scholastic Book Services.

McKee, D. 1980. *Not Now, Bernard.* London, UK: Red Fox–Random House Children's Books.

Moats, L. C. 2001. *Speech to Print: Language Essentials for Teachers.* Baltimore, MD: Paul H. Bookes.

Peregoy, S.F. and O.F. Boyle. 2004. *Reading, Writing and Learning in ESL: A Resource Book for K-8 Teachers. 4th ed.* White Plains, NY: Longman Education.

Popp, M. S. 1996. *Teaching Language and Literature in Elementary Classrooms: A Resource Book for Professional Development.* Maweh, NJ: Lawrence Earlbam.

Sileci, S. B. 2002. *Best Friends 3*. Mexico City, Mexico: McGraw-Hill/Contemporary.

Chapter **Five**

Teaching writing to young learners

Goals

At the end of this chapter, you should be able to:

 provide your own definition for *writing*.

 identify issues that impact young learners learning to write.

 distinguish between product and process as they relate to writing.

 describe the steps of the writing process.

identify techniques and activities for different steps of the writing process.

1. Introduction

The aim of this chapter is to discuss issues related to the teaching of writing to young **ESL** or **EFL** learners. The chapter begins with a description of what writing is as it relates to young learners. In the next section, background information on the teaching of writing as part of physical and cognitive development is provided. Next, the commonly used steps of process writing are presented including the types of writing that children can produce in the classroom. Then, basic suggestions for implementing writing instruction are provided, and suggestions for using different types of materials to teach writing finish up the chapter.

2. What is writing?

What do you think of when the word *writing* is mentioned? You could think of writing as the act of picking up a pencil and forming letters either by printing or writing them in cursive. You could think about the act of composing a piece of text. Or you could think of writing as an act completed by someone else, as in the writings of William Shakespeare. Because writing is multifaceted, it is only logical that it evokes different images. When working with young learners, it is important to remember that along with learning how to write in English, they are refining their oral-language skills, and depending upon the age, beginning to develop written-language skills in their native language. Remember that if students don't have writing skills in their native language, they most likely will not have them in their second language. Teachers of young learners should never underestimate the value of native-language literacy.

Writing is a combination of process and product (Sokolik, 2003). The process refers to the act of gathering ideas and working with them until they are presented in a manner that is polished and comprehensible to readers. The concept that writing is a process is very useful to young writers (Olson, 2003). In my experience, young learners like to know that writing is done in steps which are as important as the steps necessary to cook something such as chicken or eggs. In addition, when "teaching writing to young children, we must recognize the complexity of the process" (Dorn and Soffos, 2001, p. 2). Young learners need to know that a final piece of writing–or the product–such as a book, has grown out of many steps which make up the process.

For a young learner, what do you think is the hardest part of writing? Do you think it is holding the pencil or do you think it is getting the ideas formulated and put down on paper?

Share your answer with a classmate or colleague.

3. Background to the teaching of writing

When you are teaching writing to children who are four to seven years old, you must consider two separate areas of development. First, do your students have the fine motor or physical skills necessary to hold a pencil firmly in their hands and form letters on paper? Second, do they have the **cognitive skills** necessary to formulate ideas and write them onto paper. The physical act of forming letters as well as the act of expressing oneself in written form are both challenging for young learners. Depending upon their development, learners may find it very frustrating to try to physically form letters, and they may not be able to put their thoughts together in a coherent whole. Therefore as their teacher, you face the considerable task of teaching them how to actually print letters, write words, and capture their ideas to put on paper.

Children enjoy experimenting with writing and putting their ideas down on paper. On page 104, you will see the different types of pieces of writing that children can produce that often feel very "grown-up" and exciting to them. This list will help you think about ways that you can integrate writing into your overall curriculum.

Native English-speaking children are usually taught how to print before being taught to write cursive letters. See Figure 1 (page 100) for examples of printed and

The students are working hard on their writing.

cursive letters. Students are taught printed letters first because they resemble letters found in books and, according to many teachers, forming printed letters is easier than forming cursive ones because they have more straight lines and complete circles. Young learners are often taught how to form letters by tracing lines, circles, semi-circles, and triangles because this preparation helps them master the formation of the shapes that are used for letters.

> **Print:** My name is Tommy.
>
> **Cursive:** *My name is Tommy.*

Figure 1 Printed and cursive letters

Children learning ESL or EFL can face additional obstacles when learning to form English-language letters. For example, they may have been introduced to cursive writing in their native language before printed writing or their native languages may be written with characters rather than letters. Also, they may be unfamiliar with words, sentences, and paragraphs that are written from left to right. For young learners who are just beginning to learn how to write in English or who write letters and/or characters in a different direction, teachers often put an arrow running from left to right at the top of the page to show them where to start writing.

Reflection

1. How did you learn to form letters or characters in your native language? Did you use big fat crayons? Did you use a brush?

2. How would you teach a young learner from your country to form and print letters in English?

Share your answers with a classmate or colleague.

A question that often comes up is whether to allow children to use word processors and computers to produce their written work. My feeling is that computer-generated text can be very useful for learners, particularly after they have produced their final draft. However, the ability to write words down using their own hand is an invaluable skill. Learning how to form letters is also an important aspect of motor skills development that should not be overlooked in favor of introducing children to word processors at an early age.

4. The development of writing skills

Process writing helps native English-speaking children as well as EFL or ESL young learners develop English-language writing skills. Process writing is especially appropriate for ESL or EFL young learners because one of the prominent features is an emphasis on **fluency.** Just as young children learn to speak fluently, they also need to learn how to write fluently (Cameron, 2001). The process writing approach involves the process–steps necessary to produce a good quality final piece of writing. As a teacher of writing, you need to balance the role of the process and the importance of the product. The process begins by thinking about what is going to be written (choosing a topic) and collecting ideas both formally and informally. (See Figure 2 for a list of the steps of the writing process.) The final step is to **publish.** The broad definition of publish is to make public. A piece of writing is *published* when it's put it into a form which can be formally shared with others. This final stage emphasizes the product–the result of all of the previous steps and adheres to conventions of standard spelling and grammar. Sometimes parents and occasionally even young learners themselves will want to get straight to the product and minimize the process.

In addition, it is often the case that you will be working with learners whose native language writing class has a slightly different writing emphasis from yours. For example, the children may be expected to focus entirely on correct spelling and perfect penmanship rather than on the message. I have found that children learn to accept the different writing expectations that exist between the English-language and native-language programs. My learners understand that my focus is on all aspects of the process and not just the final product.

Reflection

Think about the different types of writing assignments that you had when you were a young learner. They could have been assignments in English or another language. What was the emphasis? Was the emphasis on the process or the product?

Share your answer with a colleague or classmate.

The steps that I follow when I teach children how to use a process approach to writing are summarized in Figure 2. These steps are very similar to those followed by many teachers throughout the world teaching process writing to native and non-native speakers.

Prewrite
In this important first step, children are given an opportunity to prepare to write and to collect their thoughts and ideas. If done properly, it can ease children into writing without any hesitation or worry.

Write
Children write down all of their ideas. They do not worry about form or correctness or even the order. The objective is to get the ideas on paper as quickly as possible.

Revise
The initial piece of writing is examined and reworked so that the ideas are logical and flow together.

Edit
Learners (with the help of their teachers, caregivers, or classmates) proofread their work to make sure that there are not any content errors or grammatical or spelling errors.

Publish
The writing piece is rewritten in a published or presentable form, in a student-made book, on special paper, and/or on a computer so that it can be displayed or shared.

Figure 2 Steps of the writing process

Types of written text that children can produce

One type of writing that is common in EFL classrooms is pen-pal or pen-friend letters. Pen-pal letters allow children to develop writing skills within the context of an authentic and purposeful writing activity (Berril and Gall, 2000). Other types of correspondence can also help children use writing in a meaningful way (Linse, 1998).

Children can create their own version of virtually anything that has print. In addition to pieces of correspondence, there are over a hundred different pieces of text children can write. These range from a one-word label on a poster to a novella—a mini-novel. Children who understand the concept of print can produce writing even if they are at the beginning stages of English-language development. It is important that the piece of writing be meaningful for the learner. For example, the piece of writing in Example 1 was done by a Russian-speaking young learner who can only say a handful of words in English, yet the piece of writing was very meaningful to her. The word *Winston* was carefully written and copied from a piece of text written by her mother. Although this is only one word, it was an important word for her because Winston is an American dog who sometimes stays with her. This was a very positive, albeit brief, introduction into English-language writing.

Example 1

Look at Figure 3 (page 104) for more ideas about different pieces of text children can write. Note that there is a wide variety which represent typical creative writing activities. Children will also enjoy writing text that can be classified as environmental print. For many children this is a very meaningful type of writing.

In Figure 3, you will also see a wide variety of genres—many of which are non-fiction. This list gives you an idea of the types of writing that children can produce. To make it very interesting and intriguing for young learners, you can also have them design different things with their writing. For instance, they can create their own mini-billboards announcing an upcoming field trip or student production of a play.

Address books
Advertisements
  Magazine
  Newspaper
Aerogram
Applications
Articles
  Magazine
  Newspaper
Big books
Billboards
Book reviews
Books – fiction and
  non-fiction
Brochures
Bumper stickers
Business cards
Bus passes
Buttons (such as
  campaign buttons)
Captions (such as
  those found in a
  museum)
Cartoon reviews
Cartoons
Catalogs
Chants
Charts
Commercials
  Radio
  Television
Cookbooks
Credit cards
Directions or
  instructions
Do not disturb signs
  (such as the ones
  found in hotels)

Envelopes
Father's Day cards
Finger-plays
Food (such as candy
  wrappers, cereal
  boxes, etc.)
Furniture
Get well cards
Grandparent's Day
  cards
Invitations
Jokes
Journals
Labels
  Clothing
  Equipment
Letters
Library cards
Lists
Little books
Maps
Menus
Mother's Day cards
Movies
Movie reviews
Newsletters
Newspapers
Operas
Pen-pal or
  pen-friend letters
Permission slip
  forms
Plays
Poems
Post card
Posters

Printed programs
  Plays and other
  student programs
  (such as variety
  shows)
Rhymes
Riddles
Safety cards (such as
  the ones seen on
  airplanes)
Science experiments
Science reports
Signs
Slogans
Songs
Stickers
Stories
Sympathy cards
Telephone books
Thank you cards
Tickets
  Ballet
  Bus
  Concert
  Plane
  Play
  Spaceship
  Train
Timetables
  Bus
  Plane
  Train
Titles
Tongue twisters
Toys
Verse
Word problems

Figure 3 Types of writing young learners can produce

Depending on the final product that children produce, you may utilize some or all of the steps of the writing process. For example, if children are writing a journal for their own use, then you won't need to worry about editing and publishing the writing because it is not meant to be formally shared with others. However, if you are planning a "publishing party" to which family and community members are invited, you would want to use all of the steps of the writing process and insist that the final product is as close to perfect as humanly possible.

Action

1. Look at Figure 3 and make a list of pieces of writing that seven- or eight-year-olds could produce.

2. Add any genres you think are missing from Figure 3.

Share your answer with a classmate or colleague.

The writing process: prewriting

For every piece of writing there is always a prewrite activity. If you are writing a grocery list, for example, your prewrite could be as simple as going to the refrigerator to see what you have inside. In the classroom, prewriting can be as simple as a drawing activity, or it can be woven into a discussion between the teacher and learners. Look at Extract 1, which is a prewrite activity between a teacher and a group of 10-year-old students who attend a bilingual English-Spanish school. As with all the extracts in this book, T stands for *teacher* and S stands for *student*.

Extract 1

T: *What have we been working on during writing?*

S1: *Newspaper articles.*

T: *What type of newspaper articles have we been looking at?*

S2: *All kinds.*

T: *Can someone give me an example?*

S1: *News.*

S3: *Sports.*

S4: *Food.*

T: *Good. What have the stories been about?*

S1: *Tsunami*

T: *What did we learn how to write last week?*

S2: *Titles.*

T: *That's right. What did we learn about titles or headlines?*

S4: *They shouldn't be boring.*

T: *Yes, that's right. The title needs to attract attention.*

S5: *It's gotta be interesting.*

T: *Yes. Today we are going to be writing newspaper stories. What are some different topics for newspaper articles?*

S3: *The tsunami.*

T: *Yes, that has been in the news for a long time. What else?* (Continues **brainstorming** topics of different newspaper stories, writes down their suggestions on the board.)

S5: *The really-really-really big plane with two stories.*

T: *Yes, that is a topic that newspaper readers would like to know more about. Now, I would like you to go over and look at the computer. You can see that I put up a page from the New York Times, a very important newspaper. What do you see on the screen?*

S1: *Writing and a picture.*

T: *Yes, that's exactly right. Quite often there are pictures that go with newspaper stories. Please take out your markers and your writing paper.*

S2: *What are we going to do next?*

T: *I want you to draw a box on your page like this.* (Draws a box on the board) *Very good. Now you are to draw a picture for a newspaper story.* (Points to the list on the board as a way to prompt students.)

As a prewrite, the teacher reviews what the children have been doing related to writing newspaper articles. He asks a number of questions to focus on what they have already done. Next, he asks them to think about current events. He writes down the children's ideas on the board. As a second prewriting activity, he asks the children to draw a picture for different newspaper stories. The teacher walks around the room and watches to see the students' work. Everyone in the class, even one boy who is often at a loss as to what to do, is actively engaged.

Through the prewriting activity, children have been primed so they immediately got to work. The next step is for them to write the title for their newspaper article and to begin to write the article itself. Once children have finished their drawings, they immediately launch into the writing without hesitation. The time spent on the prewriting activities has prepared them to sit down and write immediately. They show no fear of the blank page because they have been given the time and necessary guidance to gather their ideas.

1. Look at Figure 3 (page 104). Choose two types of writing your learners would like to write. If you don't currently teach young learners, choose any age group you think you will be working with.

2. Create prewriting and writing activities for the two types of writing you choose.

Share your prewriting activities with a classmate or colleague.

The writing process: writing

After you have done prewriting, the next step is to get thoughts and ideas down on paper. For instance, if a child is going to be writing a manual on how to use her favorite toy, she could write down the steps she does when she plays with it. At this point, it doesn't matter if she leaves out a step or repeats herself. The point is to get the thoughts down on paper. Young learners need to know that at this point in the writing process, they can write down any idea related to the topic. The ideas can be rearranged, added to, and edited later on. Some young learners may get silly and write things that they think are funny but completely unrelated to the writing topic. These young learners will need to be reminded that what they write must be related to the chosen topic. In addition, you can help eliminate the silliness factor if you make sure learners are writing about topics which are of interest to them. A practical note: young learners need to have enough blank paper and pencils or markers at their disposal. To facilitate rearranging information, young learners may want to write each sentence on a different index card so that they can put their sentences in a different order without having to copy everything over. Nothing should slow down the child's process and momentum.

The writing process: revising

Revising occurs when a writer looks for feedback from a teacher or another student (Vaca, Vaca, and Gove, 2000). Children, in fact most writers, have a tendency to think that once words are down on paper, they are finished writing. They also often see the teacher's role as either saying that everything is fine or being a copyeditor and fixing all spelling and grammar errors. Instead, you want to establish yourself in the role of consultant for your learners. Your role is to help them learn how to make their writing interesting and comprehensible to the reader.

You do not need to be the only person to give students feedback. Besides learning to revise on their own, their classmates, caregivers, or classroom aides can help students revise. However, at this stage, most teachers do review their students' work. Your comments should focus on content and not grammatical or spelling errors. Children need to know what ideas or organization they should keep, as well as what they should change. Praise as well as suggestions for improvement should be specific. Finally, your feedback should both compliment and provide suggestions where the student came make improvements.

Look at Example 2. It is the piece of writing that goes with the Talking and Writing Box described on page 11. The prompt or suggestion for writing is *Which item on your box makes you smile? Why?* The sample piece of writing is from a six-year-old who has been studying English for two years.

Example 2

The puppy makes me smile. Puppies are nice.

Extract 2

T: Your first sentence tells the reader one of the reasons why you like puppies. It is a good beginning. Why else do you like puppies?

S: Well. Um. They're cute.

T: Do you know any puppies?

S: Yeah.

T: Can you tell me anything else about the puppy that you know?

S: Well. Um. My puppy is happy when I come home.

T: What is your puppy's name?

S: Argos.

T: You have a really good beginning. Why don't you write about Argos and how Argos feels when you come home?

S: OK.

Note that the teacher started by telling the student exactly what she liked about the student's writing. This is helpful information for the learner. It wouldn't have been nearly as helpful if she had simply said that it was good. Eventually you will want to teach learners how to revise their writing on their own as well as how to help their peers revise their writing.

Action

1. Look at the following comments made by teachers to help students revise pieces of writing. Indicate if each one would be useful to the student.

   A. I really liked your poem.

   B. I was confused because your first and second sentence didn't seem to match. In the first sentence you wrote, *Mrs. Tooley only had a big potato.* Then you wrote, *Mrs. Tooley ate a big carrot.* You may want to rewrite the sentences so that they follow each other.

C. I liked the way you used the words *too loud* and *bark* in your poem. I could almost hear the dog!

D. It didn't make sense. I couldn't understand anything that you were talking about.

E. There were at least five different errors. I was very discouraged by them. You should just try harder.

F. I noticed that you forgot to capitalize the names of people. People are important, so their names start with big or capital letters. It would help me as a reader if you remember to use capital letters. This way I will know when you are talking about a specific person.

2. If you thought a comment from above would not be useful, explain to a classmate or colleague why it would not be useful. Then revise the comment to make it more helpful.

The writing process: editing

Children have a hard time accepting that editing is necessary. They are very honest about how painful it can be to rework a piece they feel is already finished. As one young learner explained, "I don't think anyone will notice the mistakes."

Correcting children's errors and helping children find and correct their own errors presents a real dilemma for teachers. On one hand, you do not want to dampen their enthusiasm for writing. On the other hand, they need to know how to write using standard conventions of spelling, grammar, and punctuation. Sometimes I let children use a red pen so they can correct their own mistakes. Other times, I tell children they are to go on a scavenger hunt (see page 130) through their own writing to count how many times they used a period or capital letter the correct way. Checklists which tell students what to look for in their own writing as well as in the work of their peers can also be very useful. For instance, you can have a checklist that reminds students to make sure that all of the names of people have been capitalized. An item on a checklist could also remind students to make sure that the story has a good beginning.

The writing process: publishing

After a piece of writing has been edited, it is ready to be published. Publishing refers to putting the writing in a final finished format where it can be shared with others. Publishing can be a great motivator for young learners. For example, young learners might write poems about the rain that they encountered on their way to school. The children then could publish their poems on raindrop-shaped paper and hang them from the ceiling as mobiles. Or children could make posters with suggestions for doing homework and decorate them with drawings or pictures cut out of magazines.

What are some ways to publish different pieces of student writing? Think about student-produced literature as well as non-fiction.

Share your answer with a classmate or colleague.

5. Classroom techniques and activities

Implementing a process approach to writing can easily be done in both ESL or EFL classrooms with young learners. The amount of time that you devote to the development of writing skills will depend upon the overall objectives of your program. Regardless of the program objectives, children should be given opportunities and encouragement to jot their ideas down. Several techniques and activities for implementing different aspects of process writing are discussed in this section.

Writing models

Good writers are readers, and good writers read both fiction and non-fiction. Thus, you want to provide reading material that will model the type of writing your young learners will produce. By reading and exposing children to a variety of good fiction and non-fiction, you are helping them become better writers. In addition to books, magazines, and newspapers, be sure to include the types of environmental print in Figure 3 (page 104).

Student-made reports, such as the one included in Example 3, can serve as a good model for young writers.

Example 3

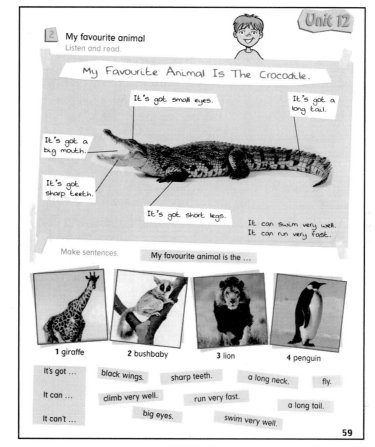

Excellent Book 1 (Bradshaw and Hadfield, 2003, p. 59)

The textbook page in Example 3, designed for six- or seven-year-old children, models writing a non-fiction report about crocodiles. The model can serve as a prewrite for children to write about their favorite animal and shows how to publish writing with a combination of text and illustration.

Favorite stories can also be used as a model. Children can be eased into writing their own stories by reading a story and then writing the prequel or sequel. For example, you could ask your learners to write a sequel to "Goldilocks and the Three Bears" (pages 34 and 35). Their story could be titled, *Goldilocks Gets Punished* or *Goldilocks Doesn't Get Punished*. After reading or rereading the original story, you could have a prewriting discussion where you prompt your learners with questions such as, *What do you think the three bears should do to Goldilocks? Do you think that they should talk to Goldilocks' parents? Why or why not? What do you think her parents should do to her?* You then ask your students to write their sequel.

Group writing

Children can work collaboratively on a writing project, but it needs to be carefully organized on the part of the teacher. You might begin group writing by doing a language experience approach story as seen on page 85. The language experience approach is used to teach children reading but can also be used to introduce writing and group writing. You can show children how different members of the class contributed to a group story by writing the child's initials next to each line he contributed.

You can also have young learners create a group book. For example, they could author different pages about their favorite things. Each page could have the same sentence starter such as, "My favorite things are _____." The children then finish each sentence and illustrate it.

Young learners can also work in small groups to create different pieces of written text. For example, if students are writing a science report, two children could conduct a simple experiment and the third child could write down what is occurring as it occurs. Once the experiment has been completed, the three can get together and rewrite, edit, and publish the science report.

Talking and Writing Box

The Talking and Writing Box described on page 11 can be used as part of your writing program. The creation of the box is a prewriting activity in and of itself. For a writing activity, you can give students a prompt or suggestion about what to write. You may also want to model the activity by following different prompts and writing about your own Talking and Writing Box. Children may want to keep their writing about their Talking and Writing Box in a small notebook stored within the box itself.

Writing centers

A writing center can be set up in most classrooms. If you share a classroom with other teachers or move from room to room, your writing center can be stored in a file folder box and pulled out and set up when you enter the room. A writing center with brightly colored pens and papers will often inspire children to write. The writing center can be used to inspire learners at every step of the writing process, as well as to help them develop the fine motor skills necessary to produce neat and legible writing. The writing center should be placed in a clean, cheery place that invites children to compose different pieces of writing. If possible, a computer that includes a word processor can also be included in the center.

The writing center can be used by children at any stage of the writing process. They can use it as a place to start pieces of writing or as a place to "publish" their writing. The writing center can also be used for writing conferences between the teacher and a student or between two classmates.

Writing conferences

One common and very useful way to help children with revising is with writing conferences. There can be one conference per piece of writing, or there can be a series of conferences for a specific piece of writing. There will also be times when a student produces a piece of writing without any conferences. These can be held between teacher and learner or between learners themselves. They can be brief, two or three minutes in length, or longer, up to half an hour. They should always be focused first on the content. Subsequent conferences can deal with conventions of print. In order to work effectively, children need to be taught how to comment and critique their own writing and that of their peers.

Inventive spelling

Invented spelling refers to students' attempts at spelling words based on their developing cognitive and literacy skills. Invented spelling can reveal valuable information about the child's English-language literacy development (Tompkins, 2000).

Example 4 has two pieces of inventive spelling and explanations of each.

Example 4

Dis es mi haws. = This is my house.

Young learners may have trouble distinguishing between *th* and *da* sounds. The spelling patterns may reflect the difficulties they have pronouncing the different words.

Wad da ya want? = What do you want?

This reflects reduced speech which is very common among native speakers. Although the child would hear the question as one word, *Waddayawant?*, she has recognized the fact that the words should be separated.

Inventive spelling has received a great deal of attention in recent years, not all of it positive. Some argue that inventive spelling harms children's ability to spell. However, I believe watching the children's thought processes with regard to their inventive spelling is very valuable. I also do not want to slow children down and interfere with the expression of their ideas when they are in the *write* stage of the writing process. When it comes to the editing and publishing stages of the process, then it is important to pay attention to spelling.

Word Walls

Word Walls are lists of words that the children have encountered in their reading and that can be used in their writing. These lists should be posted on the walls of your classroom—hence their name. Learners can refer to a Word Wall during various stages of the writing process. Different Word Walls can have different focuses. For instance, one Word Wall could include high-frequency words that learners often see in their reading. The words can be arranged alphabetically. Other Word Walls can be arranged topically. If you arrange a Word Wall according to different topics or subjects, you might want to color code them.

Action

1. Make a Word Wall list of 20 high-frequency words 10-year-old children might use.

2. Make a Word Wall list of 20 words for a topic that 10-year-old children might use. You may even want to look at a student book designed for 10-year-old children before deciding upon your topic.

Share your answers with a classmate or colleague.

6. Writing in the classroom

More and more young learners' coursebooks are including a writing component. For young learners under the age of five, emphasis is often placed on the formation of the letters themselves. For older learners, content area coursebooks designed for native English speakers are used more often in ESL or EFL classrooms. They often have English-language writing activities related to the content that learners may be studying in English or in their native language.

Look at Example 5. It is a page designed for four- or five-year-old young learners. This page is aimed at helping children develop the fine motor skills required to write English-language letters.

Example 5

[Image of tracing worksheet with candles on a cake]

> **6** Unit 2
>
> **Tracing straight and curved lines**
> Review vocabulary: *cake, candles*. Trace the lines on the candles and the cake. Count the candles.

Fingerprints First Letters 2 (Linse and Schottman, 2000, p. 6)

Reflection

What are students expected to do on the page in Example 5? How will it help learners develop English-language writing skills?

Share your answers with a classmate or colleague.

Content area writing activities for young learners

More and more writing activities for young learners are finding their way into content area coursebooks designed for native English-speaking children. One reason for this is that children have conceptual knowledge in their native language which they are proud of and can transfer into English.

Example 6 (page 116) is from a science book designed for eight- or nine-year-old children. The students have been studying about the way that the Earth changes with events such as earthquakes and volcanoes. Some of the pages and even writing activities can easily be adapted for use with ESL or EFL children.

Example 6

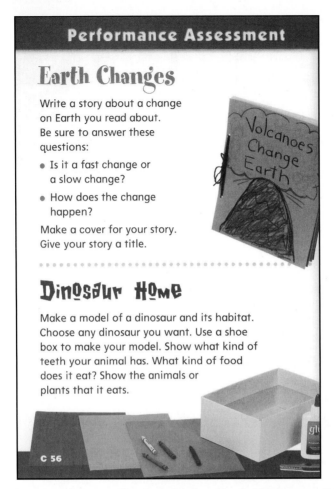

McGraw-Hill Science (Grade 2 Student Book 2001, page C 56)

Let's look at how a teacher could use Example 6 in every step of the writing process. As a prewriting activity, children can brainstorm all of the different ways that the Earth can change. As a writing activity, they can select one topic and answer the questions on the page. As a revision activity, they can participate in a writing conference with their teacher or classmate. As an editing activity, they can refer to a Word Wall for science words related to the topic. As a publishing activity, they can make little books about different natural events such as volcanoes and earthquakes.

Surprisingly, math books are also including writing activities for young learners. These activities can help children develop higher-order thinking skills as well as writing skills. For the fourth activity in Example 7, students are supposed to make up a story about the numbers.

Example 7

Problem Solving Practice

Name_____

Solve.

① There are 217 crayons in the box.

Write how many hundreds, tens, and ones in 217.

hundreds	tens	ones

② Write how many hundreds, tens, and ones in 439.

_____ hundreds _____ tens _____ ones

Write the number that is 100 more than 439.

_____

③ Write the word name for 793.

_____

Write the word name for the number that is 10 less than 793.

_____

🖉 **Write a Story!**

④ Write the number 962 in expanded form. Then write a story about 962 stickers.

_____ + _____ + _____

_____

Chapter 21   Problem Solving Practice   four hundred nine **409**

Problem Solving

McGraw-Hill Math (Grade 2 Student Book 2001, page 409)

Action

1. Write a prewriting activity that you could have young learners do for Example 7, #4.

2. What are four publishing activities that could be done with this page?

Share your answers with a classmate or colleague.

7. Conclusion

This chapter began with a discussion of the different meanings of the word *writing*. Writing as a process and a product were discussed as well as the physical act of forming letters. The different steps or stages of a process used to produce pieces of written text were explored. Attention was paid to helping children become excited about writing by creating pieces of written text that are representative of different genres ranging from cereal boxes to stories. Specific suggestions for teaching and modeling writing were also provided for learners at different stages of language and literacy development, and a wide range of written products that children can produce were also included.

Further readings

Dorn, L.J. and C. Soffos. 2001. *Scaffolding Young Writers: A Writers' Workshop Approach.* Portland, ME: Stenhouse Publishers.

This useful book provides suggestions for supporting young learners as they develop beginning writing skills. It follows the principles of developmentally appropriate instruction.

Tompkins, G.E. 2000. *Teaching Writing: Balancing Product and Product.* Upper Saddle River, NJ: Prentice Hall, Pearson.

This book provides a very comprehensive treatment of the issues related to teaching writing to young children. Although the book is targeted for teachers working with native English speakers, the information is pertinent for teachers working with EFL/ESL learners.

Helpful Web sites

National Council of Teachers of English (www.ncte.org)

This is the site of the National Council of Teachers of English. They provide information for teachers who work with school-age learners as well as university students on how to teach and encourage writing. Although the organization was originally designed for teachers working with native speakers, it has branched out and now also takes into account the needs of learners who speak languages other than English at home.

National Writing Project (www.writingproject.org)

This site was developed by the U.S.-based National Writing Project. It is designed for teachers who work with learners of all ages and provides different information on the teaching of writing. Both research-based and practice-oriented publications are available for free online.

References

Berril, D.P. and M. Gall. 2000. *Penpal Programs in the Primary Classroom.* Markham, ON, Canada: Pemroke Publishers.

Bradshaw, C. and J. Hadfield. 2003. *Excellent Book 1.* Harlow, UK: Pearson, Longman.

Cameron, L. 2001. *Teaching Languages to Young Learners.* Cambridge, UK: Cambridge University Press.

Dorn, L.J. and C. Soffos. 2001. *Scaffolding Young Writers: A Writers' Workshop Approach.* Portland, ME: Stenhouse Publishers.

Linse, C. 1997. *The Treasured Mailbox: How to Use Authentic Correspondence with Children in Grades K–6.* Portsmouth, NH: Heinemann Educational Books.

Linse, C. and E. Schottman. 2002. *Fingerprints First Letters 2.* Oxford, UK: Macmillan Educational Books.

McGraw-Hill Math 2nd Grade Student Book 2001. New York, NY: McGraw-Hill.

McGraw-Hill Science 2nd Grade Student Book 2001. New York, NY: McGraw-Hill.

Olson, C.B. 2003. *The Reading/Writing Strategies for Teaching and Learning in the Secondary Classroom.* Boston, MA: Allyn and Bacon.

Sokolik, M. 2003. Writing. In D. Nunan (ed.), *Practical English Language Teaching* New York, NY: McGraw-Hill, 87–107.

Tompkins, G.E. 2000. *Teaching Writing: Balancing Product and Product.* Upper Saddle River, NJ: Prentice Hall, Pearson.

Vaca, J.L., R.T. Vaca, and M.K. Grove. 1995. *Reading and Learning to Read.* New York, NY: HarperCollins.

Chapter **Six**

Teaching vocabulary to young learners

1. Introduction

The aim of this chapter is to consider a number of issues related to the teaching of vocabulary. First, I provide explanations of what vocabulary is as well as background information which will help you as you plan an oral- and/or written-language program. The vocabulary teaching principles which have emerged in recent years are presented next. In addition, I provide a range of techniques which can be used to teach vocabulary to young learners.

2. What is vocabulary?

Language consists of words. Vocabulary is the collection of words that an individual knows. A six-year-old speaker who has a very well-developed vocabulary for someone her age in her native language might know the words *abstract* and *dynamic*. Alternatively, you might say that a six-year-old who doesn't know the words *rectangle* and *home* has an extremely limited vocabulary. Very young children learn vocabulary items related to the different concepts they are learning. When children learn numbers in their native language, they are adding numerical concepts as well as vocabulary items. Colors are another example of vocabulary items which also represent conceptual knowledge.

Coursebooks for young learners often emphasize nouns because they are easy to illustrate and because often young learners don't have literacy skills, so the only words that can easily be featured are nouns. It is important to remember that even though nouns are important, vocabulary is more than just nouns. As a teacher, it is important that you include verbs, adjectives, adverbs, and prepositions as part of your vocabulary curriculum. In addition, you will want to include different **lexical** fields such as colors, days of the week, and action verbs. You will also want to make sure that children add these words to their receptive and expressive vocabularies.

It is important to help young learners expand their vocabularies through formal and informal instruction. For formal instruction, you will want to teach students the meanings of words and ways to uncover the meaning of words through direct instruction. Informal instruction is non-rule oriented and often a "by the way" approach.

3. Background to the teaching of vocabulary

Vocabulary development is an important aspect of language development and the research that has been conducted in recent years is very exciting. A variety of studies have proven that appropriate vocabulary instruction benefits language students, especially school-age learners. According to McKeown and Beck (2003) it is important to use both formal and informal vocabulary instruction that engages students' **cognitive skills** and gives opportunities for the learners to actually use the words. You want students to use thinking skills such as analyzing which of two words would be a better choice in a sentence. An example would be having a child choose between the words *enormous* and *giant* in a sentence about sandwiches. You also want to give learners opportunities to use the words by playing games or responding to complex questions that include the words.

Having different learning opportunities will help improve learners' overall language ability by improving their vocabulary. In other words, the "goal is for students to become word-savvy, to develop an understanding of how words work within the context of reading and writing, and to become excited about words as they learn to manipulate them in playful ways" (Brand, 2004. p. 4).

Teachers should facilitate vocabulary learning by teaching learners useful words and by teaching strategies to help learners figure out meanings on their own (Nation, 2003). Useful words are words that children are likely to encounter—words that occur in a **high frequency.** Useful words are also words which are of interest and intriguing to children. To a young learner interested in cooking, the words *recipe* and *ingredient* could be very useful as well as meaningful. To a young learner interested in machines, the words *gear* and *lever* could be very useful and meaningful.

Learners need to acquire vocabulary learning strategies in order to discover the meaning of new words. The strategies should be useful within the classroom as well as when learners are in a situation where they encounter new and unfamiliar words on their own. The strategies should also help children acquire new vocabulary words that they hear and see.

Vocabulary should be integrated into teaching the four skills—listening, speaking, reading, and writing. For example, you might include vocabulary items as part of a **Total Physical Response** listening activity. As another vocabulary activity, you could introduce students to specific lexical items that they would encounter as part of their reading lesson. To help students add words to their written vocabularies, you could encourage them to refer to a Word Wall (page 114) when they are producing different pieces of written text.

4. Principles for teaching vocabulary

A number of principles can be helpful when focusing on vocabulary development as part of an **ESL** or **EFL** program. The principles addressed below apply to young learners at various stages of English-language development. They can be used to help learners develop oral- and written-language skills. In programs where children have not yet gained literacy skills in their native language, you will want to focus on oral-language vocabulary development.

Emphasize both direct and indirect teaching.

Direct and indirect vocabulary instruction should be included as part of a vocabulary development program (Carlo et al., 2004). **Direct instruction** refers to teaching the words and their meanings. An example of direct instruction would be pre-teaching vocabulary items students will encounter in a reading selection. **Indirect instruction** refers to helping children learn appropriate strategies so they can figure out the meaning of words on their own. For example, teaching the prefixes *uni*, *bi*, and *tri* to students and then having them point to pictures of a unicycle, bicycle, and tricycle.

Reflection

When you were a child in school, how did you learn vocabulary items? What strategies did your teacher teach to remember vocabulary words or to figure out what a word meant without using a dictionary?

Teach vocabulary words before a new activity.

When vocabulary words are taught before a new activity, students benefit in two ways. First, they are better able to comprehend the activity. Second, teaching vocabulary words in advance makes it more likely that students will actually acquire the target vocabulary words (National Institute of Child Health and Human Development, 2000). This principle holds true for stories (oral and written), songs, and many other language-rich activities.

Extract 1 (page 124) is from a lesson used to introduce bugs. This lesson is being taught to a group of six-year-olds who are going to be reading about different bugs. This portion of the lesson is focusing on the **pre-teaching** of vocabulary items that learners will need when they read the book. As with all extracts in this book, T stands for *teacher* and S stands for *student*.

> **T:** *Today I brought in some bugs. They're in my bag. Do you want to see them?*
>
> **Ss:** *Yes!*
>
> **T:** *OK. Who wants to come up and pick out a bug?*
>
> **Ss:** *Me. Me. (Hands go up all over the room.)*
>
> **T:** *All right, Tiho, you can pull one out.*
>
> **S1:** *Ooh. (Pulls out a plastic spider.)*
>
> **T:** *Does anyone know what it is?*
>
> **S2:** *Spider.*
>
> **T:** *Yes, that's right. Everyone. What is it? (Teacher emphasizes, What is it.)*
>
> **Ss:** *It's a spider.*
>
> **T:** *That's right. It's a spider. Everyone.*
>
> **Ss:** *It's a spider.*
>
> **T:** *Now I need someone else? OK, Suh.*
>
> **S3:** *Ooh. I know. I know. Ladybug.*
>
> **T:** *Very good. Everyone. What is it?*
>
> **Ss:** *It's a ladybug.*
>
> **T:** *All right. Who's next?*

The teacher used the bag as a way to stimulate student interest in the words that she was pre-teaching. She then let the children "discover" the different types of bugs. She had them respond in complete sentences because it helped the learners to remain interested in the lesson.

Teach how to use context clues appropriately.

Students can benefit from learning how to use **context clues** and guessing the meaning from the **context** (Decarrico, 2001). This is a strategy that learners can use when they encounter unfamiliar words. Conversely, Beck and McKeown (2003) point out that in addition to teaching how to use context clues, students also need to be taught that context clues do *not* always help readers to understand the meanings of unfamiliar words. Children need to be taught that there are times, especially when reading, when they will *not* be able to figure out the meaning from context clues.

Extract 2 is from a class of 10-year-olds who have been studying English for about two years. The children have been reading some challenging material. The teacher is showing the students that there are times when you can use context clues to figure out the meaning of unfamiliar words. She is also showing that there are times when the context clues do not provide enough information to figure out the meaning of the unfamiliar word.

Extract 2

T: Today we are going to read some sentences. There are some unfamiliar words. We are going to try to figure out the meaning of the unfamiliar words by using clues that are around the words. All right, Sindi, please read the first one.

S1: The grandmother found some cherries, figs, apples, and pears on the table.

T: Does anyone know what figs are?

S2: Fruit.

T: How did you know?

S2: Well everything else in the list is fruits, so it made sense that figs would be, too.

T: Excellent. You used context clues or the words around figs to figure out that figs are a fruit. All right, Neli, please read the next one.

S3: She found a dove next to the fruit.

T: Very good sounding out of the word dove. Does anyone know what a dove is? (The students shake their heads NO.) Let's see if we can figure it out.

S4: It is a toy.

T: No, Jon, it isn't a toy. Let's read the sentence again together.

Ss: She found a dove next to the fruit.

T: Do you have any ideas?

S2: A knife.

T: Why do you think a knife?

S2: So that she can cut the fruit.

T: An excellent guess. It is always good to guess. However, let me tell you something important. This is an example of a time when context won't help you. There isn't enough information in the sentence to figure out the meaning of the unfamiliar word.

S4: What is a dove?

T: Since you can't figure it out in the sentence, what could you do?

S3: (with a groan) Use the dictionary.

T: That's right.

Present multiple exposures to new vocabulary items.

Young learners make educational gains when they are exposed to vocabulary items repeatedly in rich contexts (National Institute of Child Health and Human Development, 2000). In other words, you shouldn't expect that a vocabulary word taught on Monday will be remembered on Wednesday. As part of your teaching repertoire, remember that a new word should reappear many times and in different situations for the next several weeks of instruction.

Learners also benefit when there is multi-sensory vocabulary input. For instance, if you are teaching children about rooms in a house, on Monday you could bring in doll furniture for each room and have children guess what rooms the furniture goes in. On Wednesday, you could play different vocabulary games with picture cards featuring rooms in a house. The next week, you might have a puppet show where the puppets are moving into a new house. Another example would be if your students are studying the names of different animals. For the first lesson, they could sing songs with the different names. Later in the week, your learners could make pictures of animals. While they are drawing, you could walk around the classroom and ask, "What animal is that?" Not only will the child who is drawing the duck repeat the word *duck*, but all of the children around him will hear the word and associate it with a picture of a duck.

Give opportunities for *deep processing* of vocabulary items.

Deep processing means working with information at a high cognitive and/or personal level. Deep processing makes it more likely that information will be remembered. Part of deep processing is having students establish connections between new words and their prior knowledge. Simply memorizing lists of words and their meanings is not adequate for students to integrate the vocabulary words into their personal vocabularies.

Deep processing is a very important component of vocabulary acquisition and development. It is also closely related to reading and reading comprehension (Blachowicz and Fisher, 2000) and to overall language development. Deep processing refers to using words in contexts which are especially meaningful to the learner. This can involve grouping words according to different characteristics or attributes. It can also involve relating the words to your learners' own lives. Personalizing vocabulary lessons will greatly help students' deep processing. For example, if you teach the above lessons on rooms in a house, you may want to end the unit by having students talk about or write sentences about the rooms in their houses.

Teach students to use dictionaries.

The use of dictionaries as a tool for EFL and ESL instruction has come back into style (Thornbury, 2002). Young learners can benefit from using dictionaries. Very young children, under the age of six, can use a picture dictionary where words are grouped into different categories. Children who are at the beginning stages of language and literacy development can also use picture dictionaries as a tool to help them increase both their vocabulary knowledge and their use of context clues. For example, if children are learning about grapefruit, they can be guided to a picture dictionary page topically arranged to include fruit. They will discover the grapefruit as being a fruit.

Learners with English-language literacy skills can also use dictionaries where the words are placed in alphabetical order. As a teacher, it is important to teach children how to use different dictionaries. For example, most students need to be told that the first meaning given in a dictionary is the most common. In addition, students who use electronic dictionaries need to be cautioned regarding their limitations.

Have students keep vocabulary notebooks.

Vocabulary notebooks provide students with opportunities to develop a variety of vocabulary acquisition strategies and also help students have more control over their learning (Fowles, 2002). Children who are in the beginning stages of language and literacy development can create their own picture dictionaries while older learners can make more sophisticated notebooks and dictionaries. Young learners can be given old address books written with Latin letters. They are already perforated with tabs for most of the English-language letters. Children can easily record new words that they are learning. For example, the learners doing the lesson in Extract 2 (page 125) could add the word *dove* in their vocabulary notebook. This is a strategy that learners should be encouraged to do on their own.

| Example 1

5. Classroom techniques and activities

Many different approaches and activities can be used to help children develop their vocabularies. It is important that you include vocabulary items that are part of the curriculum as well as provide learners with opportunities to work with items they find meaningful.

Connecting vocabulary to young learner's lives through personalization

Ask children questions that will help them to relate new words to their own lives. This will help them to remember the words and hopefully will help them to use the words in their own speech and writing. Questions used to prompt vocabulary development should be carefully phrased to help learners develop their cognitive skills. Look at the questions in Figure 1. Note that the target vocabulary item is written in italics and that there are words for beginning and advanced students.

Which *farm* animal would you like to take home?
What is your favorite way to *move*—jump, hop, skip, etc.?
What is the most important piece of *furniture* in your house?
If you were to have any *zoo* animal as a pet, which one would it be?
When you are *hungry*, what do you want to eat?
What makes you feel *happy*?
What make you feel *irritated*?

Figure 1 Questions to prompt vocabulary development

These questions are designed to prompt learners to really think about the words. Whenever possible, the questions should allow learners to relate the words to their own lives. Also, to encourage cognitive skills, point out that this is a good strategy for remembering new words. The questions should also help learners develop higher-order thinking skills by having them analyze information in order to answer the questions.

Action

Make a list of questions for the vocabulary items: *car, house, dog, gift, yellow, leaf, five, time, season, help, work.* Use Figure 1 as a model.

Share your answers with a classmate or colleague.

Word for the day

Select a specific word you will focus on each day. You can pre-select the word, or you can have your learners decide what word will be featured. For example, if children are studying jungle animals, they could learn a different species each day, or you could ask each child to bring a new word relating to the jungle on their special vocabulary day. Then when you take attendance, instead of having children say *here* they can say the word of the day. Also when children are waiting for the bell to ring, you can ask one or two of them to use the word of the day in a sentence.

Categories

Have each learner create a set of picture cards or word cards with different vocabulary items on them. Have them put one vocabulary item on each card. As they are working on their sets of cards, walk around and discuss the different words. Children who are four to seven years old can easily cope with 16–20 words, while older children can cope with up to 40 words for this activity. You can then ask your students to sort the words into two to five different categories of their own choosing. Then have them explain how they put the categories together. For younger or less advanced students, you may want to allow an *other* or *miscellaneous* category that learners can put a few in.

Example 2 shows how an 11-year-old may sort a set of words. Note that there are some words that could easily go into either category. It is important the categories are somewhat correct and make sense for the learner.

Example 2

Related to water	Related to land
harbor	railroad
water	travel
chilly	mountainous
ocean	train
sea-sick	climb
aqua	valley
ship	
foam	
shark	
octopus	
sail	
windy	

Look at a picture dictionary and randomly select 30 vocabulary items. If you do not have access to a picture dictionary, make a list of 30 nouns you'd expect to be taught in a primary or kindergarten English-language program. Write each word on a different index card. Practice putting them into four or five different categories.

Tell a classmate or colleague how and why you made your choices.

Scavenger hunt

Give children who are six years old or older an EFL or ESL coursebook that is appropriate for their age and language level. Give them a word to find in the book, such as *apple*. Young learners have to use cognitive skills to determine which unit the word would be found in. This helps learners classify words according to different categories. For children who do not have literacy skills, you can simply show them a picture of the target word. For other learners, you can write the target word on the board. Have children tell you the path they took to find the word. Note that the word should be listed on several different pages. At the end of the lesson, you or a student volunteer should write all of the page numbers on the board.

What's missing?

Place 12–20 picture or word cards on a table or the floor. Have your students look at the cards for a minute. Then have them close their eyes. Remove one card. Ask the group or an individual learner to tell you which card was removed. To make the game more challenging and interesting, have children describe the picture or word card that was removed. By describing what has been removed, your learners use more advanced higher-order thinking skills.

Mystery words

Read or say a sentence aloud and leave out a word. Have your children guess the mystery word–the word that has been omitted. For example, you might say, *I like to put _____ and mustard on my hot dog.*

If children come up with a word other than what you had in mind, you can tell them that it was a good guess but not what you were thinking. For example, if you say, *I wear a _____ on my head* and a learner says *cap*, you could say that you were thinking of another word but that *cap* also works. Children giving creative answers often leads to interesting discussions and discoveries. Children may be given different mystery words and asked to come up with their own sentences for their classmates to guess.

Concentration

Play Concentration with new vocabulary words. Concentration games can be made using picture and/or word cards. There should be two sets of cards. On one set, the vocabulary words should be printed or illustrated with pictures. On the other set, there should be matching pictures, definitions, the printed word, or the word used in a context-rich sentence. It's best to have a total of 16–24 cards. I like to tell students that this is a good strategy or game that they can use when they study for vocabulary tests.

When playing Concentration, the cards are placed face down on a table. The first learner turns over two cards and identifies them aloud. If they match, the learner keeps the cards. If they don't match, the words are placed back on the table face down in the same place from which they were taken. The next person then turns over two cards. The players take turns until there are no more cards on the table.

Make a list of words that you would like to teach young learners. Create a concentration game that you can use to teach the words. You can use a student coursebook to help you choose age-appropriate vocabulary.

Play the game with a classmate or colleague.

Vocabulary basket

Give each learner a word card. For young learners without literacy skills, you will want to use picture cards. For older learners, depending upon the vocabulary items, you may want to include words and pictures or just words. Have your students sit with their chairs in a circle. Every child should sit in a chair and hold their card so that the rest of the class can see it. You should stand in the middle of the circle holding a card. Call two word cards such as *apple* and *orange*. The two children holding the cards with *apple* and *orange* on them race to change seats; however, one is left standing because you sit in one of the empty chairs. In other words, you sit in one of the chairs that has been vacated. The child without a chair is left standing and calls out the next two words.

6. Vocabulary in the classroom

Example 3 is from a preschool-kindergarten coursebook. It is used with five-year-old children. The focus is on three specific vocabulary items, *doll*, *truck*, and *ball*. Each of the words would be interesting. Note how prominently these items are displayed on the page. It would be very easy to have the young learners point to each of the vocabulary items and later circle each one using a different colored crayon or marker.

Example 3

Peekaboo 1 (Charrington and Covill, 2003, p. 60)

Action

Make a list of other vocabulary activities and games which you could use to introduce and reinforce the vocabulary taught in Example 3.

Share your answers with a classmate or colleague.

Example 4

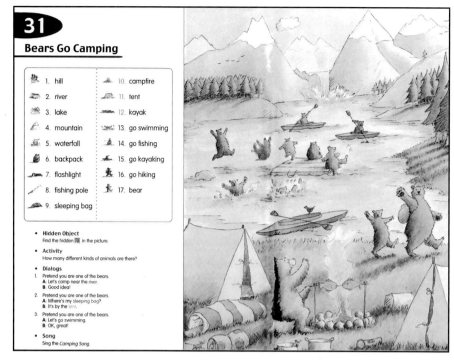

31
Bears Go Camping

1. hill	10. campfire
2. river	11. tent
3. lake	12. kayak
4. mountain	13. go swimming
5. waterfall	14. go fishing
6. backpack	15. go kayaking
7. flashlight	16. go hiking
8. fishing pole	17. bear
9. sleeping bag	

• **Hidden Object**
Find the hidden ▓ in the picture.

• **Activity**
How many different kinds of animals are there?

• **Dialogs**
1. Pretend you are one of the bears.
   A: Let's camp near the river.
   B: Good idea!

2. Pretend you are one of the bears.
   A: Where's my sleeping bag?
   B: It's by the tent.

3. Pretend you are one of the bears.
   A: Let's go swimming.
   B: OK, great!

• **Song**
Sing the *Camping Song*.

Longman Picture Dictionary (2003, Topic 31)

Picture dictionaries can be a very valuable tool. Example 4 has two pages designed for 7- to 10-year-old children with some literacy skills. The two pages could be used after learners have studied about going on a camping trip. One way to stimulate young learner interest is to play a guessing game about the different objects found in the picture. This helps learners develop higher-order thinking skills while working on vocabulary development. Extract 3 (page 134) is an example of a lesson with nine-year-old learners who have had about a year and a half of English-language instruction. The children have been learning to read and write in English. Note that both nouns and verbs are included as part of the activity.

Extract 3

T: *Please look at the picture. What do you see?*

Ss: *Bears.*

T: *What are they doing?*

S1: *Playing.*

T: *Good. That's right. Let's look under the number 31. Let's read it together.*

Ss: *Bears go camping.*

T: *Very good. What does this tell you?*

S2: *The bears are camping.*

T: *Good. Now we're going to play a game. I am going to ask you some questions, and I want you to guess the answer. I want you to guess what I am going to need to go camping. OK?*

Ss: *OK.*

T: *I am going to go camping and I want to fish. What do I need?*

Ss: *Fishing pole.*

T: *Good. What number is it?*

Ss: *8.*

T: *Good. Let's do the next one. I want to see at night. What do I need?*

Ss: *Flashlight.*

T: *Very good.*

Action

Make a list of questions that would help learners personalize the vocabulary items in Example 4. It may be difficult to come up with questions for every item, so instead, try to come up with questions for 10 items.

Share your answers with a classmate or colleague.

---

7. Conclusion

In this chapter, the word *vocabulary* was discussed as it relates to young learners. Next, vocabulary development that can take place as part of a four-skills program was explored. Basic principles of vocabulary development that apply to school-age learners were then discussed. Finally, a number of different techniques and strategies were provided that can be used with words that are selected by the teacher as well student-selected items. These techniques and strategies can be used to enrich your oral and written English-language program.

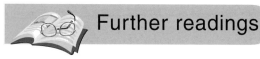

Further readings

Brand, M. 2004. *Word-Savvy: Integrating Vocabulary, Spelling and Word Study: Grades 3-6*. Portland, ME: Stenhouse Publishers.

This wonderful book provides a wealth of information about vocabulary instruction which is meaningful for learners. This title focuses on an approach which helps learners develop higher-order thinking skills.

Egan, L.H. 2001. *Best Ever Vocabulary and Word Study Games: Grades 4-8*. New York, NY: Scholastic Books.

This book provides a variety of games that will work especially well with 10- to 12-year-olds. The games helps students learn about strategies such as using context clues and prefixes and suffixes.

Helpful Web sites

Little Explorers English Picture Dictionary (www.enchantedlearning.com/dictionary.html)

This site provides pictures and very straightforward definitions for over 2,400 words. It is a very useful site for planning vocabulary lessons. Often some of the simplest words are the hardest to explain.

Word Central (www.wordcentral.com/)

Merriam Webster, the dictionary manufacturer, has put together a very useful site designed to help children develop dictionary skills, develop an appreciation for words and expand their vocabularies. This site is designed primarily for native English speakers but is especially useful for teachers working with second- and foreign-language learners.

References

Blachowicz, C. L. and P. Fisher. 2000. Vocabulary Instruction. *Handbook of Reading Research Volume III* (Kamil, M.L., P.B. Mosenthal, and R. Barr. eds.). Mahwah, NJ: Lawrence Earlbaum.

Brand, M. 2004. *Word-Savvy: Integrating Vocabulary, Spelling and Word Study, Grades 3-6*. Portland, ME: Stenhouse Publishers.

Buis, K. 2004. *Making Words Stick*. Ontario, Canada: Pembroke Publishers.

Carlo, M.S., D. August, B. McLaughlin, C.E. Snow, C. Dressler, D. Lippman, T. Lively, and C. White. 2004. Closing the gap; addressing the vocabulary needs of English language learners in bilingual and mainstream classrooms. *Reading Research Quarterly,* 39.2: 188–215.

Charrington, M. and C. Covill. 2003. *Peekaboo 1.* Oxford, UK: Macmillan Education.

Decarrico, J.S. 2001. Vocabulary learning and teaching. *Teaching English as a Second or Foreign Language. 3rd ed.* (M. Celce-Murcia ed.), Boston, MA: Heinle & Heinle.

Fowles, C. 2002. Vocabulary Notebooks: implementation and outcomes. *ELT Journal,* 54/4: 380–389.

Longman Children's Picture Dictionary. 2003. Hong Kong, PRC: Pearson Education North Asia Limited.

McKeown, M.G. and I. Beck. 2003. Chapter 2: Direct and rich vocabulary instruction. *Vocabulary instruction: Research to practice* (J. Baumann and E. Kame'eum eds.). New York, NY: Guilford Publications.

Morgan, J. and M. Rinvolucri. 2003. *Vocabulary. 2nd ed.* Oxford, UK: Oxford University Press.

National Institute of Child Health and Human Development. 2000. Chapter 4: Comprehension, Part I, Vocabulary Instruction. *Report of the National Reading Panel: Teaching children to read, an evidence-based assessment of the scientific literature on reading and its implications for reading instruction. (NIH Publication No. 00-4754).* Washington, D.C.: U.S. Government Printing Office, 4-13-4-35.

Nation, I.S.P. 2003. Vocabulary. In D. Nunan (ed.), *Practical English Language Teaching* (D. Nunan ed.). New York, NY: McGraw-Hill, 129–152.

Thornbury, S. 2002. *How to Teach Vocabulary.* Essex, UK: Pearson, Longman.

Chapter **Seven**

Assessing young learners

At the end of this chapter, you should be able to:

✔ **describe** assessment and situations where it occurs.

✔ **identify** issues you should take into account when assessing young learners.

✔ **examine** the context and situation where the assessment is taking place.

✔ **explain** ways to assess listening, speaking, reading, and writing in the classroom.

✔ **develop** assessment tools based on classroom activities.

1. Introduction

In this chapter, I will provide a summary of the latest information concerning the assessment of young language learners. We will also look at strategies, techniques, and resources you can use to assess young learners. The chapter begins with an overview of assessment and then focuses on different aspects of assessment including classroom-based assessment. We will then look at ways classroom-based assessment can be woven together or integrated with developmentally appropriate instruction for young learners. The chapter concludes with specific suggestions for using different assessment techniques in the classroom.

2. What is assessment?

Assessment occurs all the time. **Assessment** is the gathering of information for a specific purpose. When you go to a bookstore and select a book to read, you make an assessment as to which book will provide you with information or pleasure. The process is so automatic that you are probably unaware that assessment is part of it. There are other times when assessment is more conscious, such as making a decision as to which job to take or university to apply to.

Assessment differs from **evaluation.** It can be useful to look at the distinction between the two. Assessment refers to collecting information and making judgments on a learner's knowledge, whereas evaluation is used when collecting and interpreting information for making decisions about the effectiveness of an education program (Brindley, 2003).

Reflection

Think about a decision that you have made recently based on the gathering of information. It could be something like deciding what to buy for dinner or what you will do before going to sleep. Describe the decision and your thinking process when you made it.

Example
I had telephone messages from four different people this afternoon. I decided to call my boss back first because she is my boss and she expects phone calls to be returned immediately.

Share your answer with a classmate or colleague.

If you were to visit a young learner's class taught by an effective teacher, you would see the teacher automatically assessing students. You would notice the teacher paying very careful attention to her students. She would be, often unconsciously, noticing which students found the content too difficult and which ones found it too easy. Based on what she observed, she would modify her teaching. She may rephrase a question or give a student a little bit more time to answer. If a learner answered a question very quickly, she might immediately ask a more challenging question.

When we think of assessment, we usually think of teachers using it to determine how well an individual child or a group of children are doing. As a teacher, it is important to have clear instructional goals so that you can assess whether the goals have been met (Cameron, 2001). If you don't know your aims and purposes in teaching, you won't be able to determine whether they have been achieved. Assessment should reflect specific program objectives that are representative of the overall program goals.

Assessment practices should also reflect the instructional practices in place (Georgiou-Ioannou and Pavlou, 2003). If you are teaching using an approach that takes into account the developmental needs of your students, then your assessment procedures should also take into account their developmental needs. Unfortunately, there may be instances when the assessment is mandated by local or even national officials and does not correspond with the instructional practices used in the classroom.

When assessing students, it's important to remember that assessment should be a measure of what students are able to do and what they know, rather than measures of what they are not able to do and do not know (Freeman and Freeman, 2004). The emphasis should be on the skills and knowledge that students have acquired within the context of their development and cultural heritage. Assessment should help you better understand what additional skills your students need to acquire. Assessment should not just be another item on an educational "must do" list but rather should serve a real purpose ranging from initial placement to program monitoring (Brindley, 2003).

> We must make a careful distinction between constructive, classroom-rooted, best-practice forms of student evaluation and the more prevalent high-profile standardized tests that are at the center of today's education debates.
>
> Daniels and Bizar, 2004, p. 223

Assessment is different from evaluation. As mentioned above, assessment looks at what individuals and groups of learners can do. Evaluation, on the other hand, concerns an entire educational program and not just specific learners and is much wider in scope (Brindley, 2003). Much of the information you obtain from classroom assessments can, and should be, part of a program evaluation. Then when an English-language program is evaluated, effective changes can be made to improve the overall quality of the classroom.

Two concepts are important when discussing assessment. They are **validity** and **reliability.** An assessment is considered to have validity if it measures the skill it is supposed to measure with a specific group of learners. When looking to see if an assessment activity is valid, you need to look at what the activity is and what it is supposed to measure. Look at Figure 1 and note the assessment activity and the skill assessed by each activity.

Assessment Activity	Skill Assessed
Learners put all of the pictures that start with the /t/ sound together.	Phonemic awareness
Learners match a written word with the picture.	Reading / Vocabulary
Learners listen to a story and then answer comprehension questions.	Listening comprehension

Figure 1 Assessment activity and skills chart

You might want to assess if five-year-olds can correctly pronounce the /m/ sound. A valid assessment would be whether the children who have been taught the song *Do You Know the Muffin Man?* can accurately pronounce /m/ as they sing the words *muffin* and *man*. An invalid assessment of the /m/ sound would be whether they can write the letter *M* when someone says a list of words with the /m/ sound. For additional chants and fingerplays that can be used for assessment see the appendix.

When examining test validity, it is also important to determine whether the assessment is valid for the learners who will be taking the test. For instance, test items that are valid for young learners in large urban areas may not be valid for children living in rural areas. Another example would be a test which is valid for beginning learners who are 12 and 13 years old may not be valid for children who are five or six year olds.

After examining an assessment tool's validity, you should look at its reliability. An assessment tool is reliable if the results are consistent over a period of time. This means that for a test to have reliability, the results should be consistent when different teachers administer the tests and/or different teachers score them. The test results should also be consistent if they are given on different days. For example, if a test is given on two different dates and the results are very similar, then we can say that it is reliable. Of course, the results won't be identical because learners are human and won't always perform the same way on a different day or at a different time (Hughes, 1989).

3. Background to assessing young learners

Beyond validity and reliability, there are a number of additional considerations you should take into account before choosing an assessment tool to use with young learners. I will briefly discuss some important considerations.

Reasonable expectations

Make sure that the expectations for your learners are reasonable. Do not expect children to have better oral-language skills in English than they possess in their native language. For example, if children are only expressing themselves in their native language using four- and five-word sentences, they shouldn't be expected to express themselves in English using longer sentences.

Also, too often there are unrealistic expectations for children to become fluent in English. If children only have four or five hours of English a week, they shouldn't be expected to be fluent within two years. It can take five to seven years for learners to achieve academic competence in English as a second language. Don't expect that your English as a foreign language students can equal or better that. Your assessment tool should reflect the time needed to truly learn the language.

Wait time

As mentioned in Chapter 1, **wait time** is the amount of time that the teacher waits for a learner to respond to a question. When you assess students, it is especially important that you wait at least five seconds for a response. By interrupting students before they have had time to process the information and form an answer, you not only miss an assessment opportunity, but you may also be conveying the message that you don't think they know the answer. One good way to make sure that you wait five seconds is to count slowly to yourself–a thousand and one, a thousand and two, etc.

Transitioning into English

Before children are given an English-language assessment, they need time to transition into English. Language learners often walk in the classroom door thinking in their native language. I should have remembered this fact a couple of years ago when I did a demonstration assessment and lesson in Mexico. On a Monday morning, I walked into a classroom and started my assessment which included a very short warm-up writing task. The students were not on-task because they hadn't yet made the transition from Spanish, which they had spoken throughout the weekend, into English. The writing they produced was not up to their skills or ability.

If children are going to be taking English-language tests, give them a couple of minutes to transition into English before you begin the assessment. For instance, if you are working with five-year-olds, you might want to take out a puppet and have the puppet lead the class in a couple of songs. If you are working with eight- or nine-year-olds, you might want to tell them some easy English-language riddles. You can find some age-appropriate riddles by searching for *English Language Riddles* on the Internet.

Instructions to learners

Tests should assess specific aspects of language use and not if children can understand the instructions and format of the test. Unless the aim of the test is to assess if children can comprehend directions, the test should have instructions which are easy to understand. There should also be an example item which helps to clarify the instructions.

I use the following list of questions to determine if the instructions are clear:
- Are the instructions broken down into short sentences?
- Are the instructions written at or below the children's reading level?
- Is it clear what the children do first, and what they do next?
- Is all of the needed information included?
- Is the vocabulary used in the instructions appropriate for the children's age and language level?

Look at Figure 2. Note how confusing the poor instructions could be for a young learner.

Poor Instructions	Good Instructions
Look at the list of vocabulary items and circle the corresponding letter of the item which does not belong. Note that one word is dissimilar.	Look at the list of words. One word does not belong. Circle the letter of the word that does not belong.

Sample Item
a. cat
b. bird
c. house
d. fish

Figure 2 Test instructions

1. Make a list of vocabulary topics students could study—such as zoo animals, months of the year, etc.
2. Create sample vocabulary assessment items using the example in Figure 2.

Share your assessment items with a classmate or colleague.

Talking to strangers

Children are usually taught not to speak to strangers. However, there are situations when an English-language test may be given by someone who is unfamiliar to the child. Children need to be shown that the person assessing them can be trusted. This can easily be done by having the teacher or parent introduce the person administering the test to the child. This way the child will feel more comfortable and will perform better during the assessment.

4. Formal assessment

Elementary school students in most countries are required to participate in mandated **formal assessments** that assess their native language reading and math skills. In addition, young learners are increasingly being required to participate in formalized English-language testing. These tests vary greatly from country to country and often region to region within a specific country. This type of assessment may be administered on a one-to-one basis or given to a group of young learners in the form of a written test. In the case of public schools, the tests are

The boy is participating in a formal assessment.

mandated by the Ministry of Education or the state or local school district. In the case of private schools and institutes, the administration may require students to be assessed using standardized test instruments. As a teacher, if one of your students has moved from another country, you should try and obtain any assessment information that the child may have received prior to moving.

Reflection

Do you remember the first time you had to take a standardized test? How did you feel? What did your parents and teachers do to make you feel at ease?

What can a teacher do to prepare children for standardized testing so that they feel comfortable?

Share your answers with a classmate or colleague.

As a teacher, if your students are required to take standardized tests, you should ask the administration whether the test instrument and the items on the test are valid and reliable for your learners. You want to make sure that the test developer piloted the test with students who are similar to yours. It is not uncommon for private school administrators in **English as a Foreign Language (EFL)** settings to want to use **English as a Second Language (ESL)** tests to show progress. Private school administrators may feel pressured by parents to show that the progress students have made in their English-language development is comparable to the progress that ESL learners have made. Unfortunately, the tests designed for ESL have not always proven to be valid with children in EFL settings.

ESL language proficiency instruments

There are many different oral-language proficiency tests designed for use with young ESL learners in the United States. These instruments usually require someone to administer the speaking portion of the test on a one-to-one basis. These tests are used to determine if children need extra help learning English at school because they come from a home where English is not the primary language. Unfortunately, these test instruments are beginning to be used in countries where English is a foreign language—an environment they were not designed for.

Cambridge young learner assessments

In recent years, tests have been introduced for children in countries where English is a foreign language. Probably the most well-known tests are the Cambridge Young Learners Tests developed by the University of Cambridge ESOL Examinations. These tests have been piloted in many different countries with different learners to assure a high level of validity and reliability. If your EFL school insists on using a standardized test, you may want to recommend the Cambridge tests. You can go to their Web site to find out more information (see Helpful Web sites on page 163).

What should you do if you are asked to give a test that is not valid and reliable?

1. Examine the test carefully to determine some of the problem areas. For example, the test may include cultural items the students would have no way of knowing.
2. Make a list of the items that could be unfair for your learners.
3. Share your list with administrators and/or other decision makers.
4. Contact the test manufacturer to check and see if they are going to create a test which will be valid and reliable for the types of learners in your classes.
5. Look at alternative forms of assessment.

---

5. Classroom-based assessment

I like to weave assessment and instruction together and try to constantly observe my learners so that I can adjust my instruction to meet their needs. Assessment should be integrated and reflect the type of instruction taking place in the classroom. Many oral and written language activities can easily be used for classroom-based assessment. Most teaching activities can be used for assessment when there is criteria, including an aim, as well as a feedback mechanism. Before using an activity as an assessment tool, it is important to determine what type of assessment information you will gain from the activity. For instance, children may do an activity sheet where they answer questions about a story. Based on the children's answers, you can determine how well they have comprehended the story. We will now look at instructional activities which will help you to assess your students' progress in the four main language skills (listening, speaking, reading, writing). We will also look at using portfolios as assessment tools.

Listening skills

There are two main components of listening assessment in the young-learner classroom. The first is the assessment of phonemic awareness—the ability to distinguish between different sounds. The importance of **phonemic awareness** was discussed in Chapter 2. The second component of listening assessment is listening comprehension, which was also discussed in Chapter 2.

A number of different aspects of phonemic awareness can be assessed. These include the ability to distinguish between sounds, identify words that start or end with the same sound, and recognize rhyming words. When assessing phonemic awareness, you can provide children with a simple phonemic awareness assessment sheet (Example 1).

Example 1

Listen.
Circle the happy face if the sounds are the same.
Circle the sad face if the sounds are different.

Example: ☺   ☹

1. ☺   ☹
2. ☺   ☹
3. ☺   ☹
4. ☺   ☹
5. ☺   ☹

To complete the task in Example 1, children are asked to circle a happy face if the sounds are the same and a sad face if the sounds are different. For example, if you are assessing the final sounds /d/ and /t/, you could say the following words aloud: *mad/mat, bat/bad, cat/cat, hid/hit, tot/Todd, met/met.* It should be pointed out that the point of these activities is not to assess vocabulary but rather if the children can discriminate between the sounds.

Using the same worksheet, you can very easily use a different set of word pairs to assess if the children can tell if words rhyme. For example, you could read the following list aloud: *cat/mat, sand/sad, hit/hat, fill/hill, dog/dot.*

Action

Create a list of words to assess phonemic awareness. Your list can be used as the basis of assessment activities focused on beginning, medial, or final sounds. Be sure to include at least five pairs of words.

Share your list with a classmate or colleague. Discuss if you have focused on the specific sound that you were intending to assess.

When assessing listening comprehension, make sure your learners understand the individual words, instructions, and pieces of text. When assessing if children understand a specific word or phrase, ask them to point to an object or picture. For example, if you want to assess if a child comprehends the names of fruit, you could place pictures of fruit on a table and say *Please point to the banana.* If you ask your learners to point to a written word instead, you would be assessing both their listening and reading comprehension. Another way to assess their listening comprehension of fruit names would be to give all of the children in a group pictures of different pieces of fruit as in Example 2. If all of the learners know their shapes, you can then assess them by asking them to: draw a circle around the apple, draw a triangle around the banana, and draw a square around the coconut.

Example 2

You can assess learners' listening comprehension of directions by observing them as you give **Total Physical Response (TPR)** instructions. For more information on TPR see page 30. However, if you are using TPR as an assessment tool, it is essential that you only give one instruction or command at a time. It is also important that you observe children the first time a command is given, rather than when a command is repeated.

Assessing if children comprehend text they hear aloud can involve statements with pictures. For example, if children are listening to a story, you may ask "Show me what happened first. Point to the picture." or "Show me the picture of the child who was the best helper."

You can also use questions to determine if children comprehend what has been said. For instance, if you are reading a story, you can pause to ask questions about what happened in the story so far. It's important to remember that when you assess listening comprehension through the use of questions, you want to make sure that children possess the speaking skills needed to respond. For instance, you wouldn't want to ask children to describe what happened so far in the story if they did not know the past tense.

Speaking skills

Speaking skills can be assessed by asking young learners questions and engaging them in conversations. You can assess students by asking specific questions during class, as well as by talking with them on a one-to-one basis. When assessing learners' oral skills, you may want to use an analytical or holistic rubric. A **holistic rubric** provides *one* overall score. An **analytic rubric** provides information broken down into different categories.

The Student Oral Language Observation Matrix in Figure 3 is an analytic rubric used to assess speaking skills. You can use it to assess children informally, as part of your daily instruction or for formal assessment.

		1	2	3	4	5
A. Comprehension		Cannot be said to understand even simple conversation.	Has great difficulty following what is said. Can comprehend only social conversation spoken slowly and with frequent repetitions.	Understands most of what is said at slower-than-normal speed with repetitions.	Understands nearly everything at normal speech. Although occasional repetition may be necessary.	Understands everyday conversation and normal classroom discussions.
B. Fluency		Speech so halting and fragmentary as to make conversation virtually impossible.	Usually hesitant; often forced into silence by language limitations.	Speech in everyday conversation and classroom discussion frequently disrupted by the student's search for the correct manner of expression.	Speech in everyday conversation and classroom discussions generally fluent, with occasional lapses while the student searches for the correct manner of expression.	Speech in everyday conversation and classroom discussions fluent and effortless; approximating that of a native speaker.
C. Vocabulary		Vocabulary limitations so extreme as to make conversation virtually impossible.	Misuse of words and very limited vocabulary; comprehension quite difficult.	Student frequently uses wrong words, conversation somewhat limited because of inadequate vocabulary.	Student occasionally uses inappropriate terms and/or must rephrase ideas because of lexical inadequacies.	Use of vocabulary and idioms approximate that of a native speaker.
D. Pronunciation		Pronunciation problems so severe as to make speech virtually unintelligible.	Very hard to understand because of pronunciation problems. Must frequently repeat in order to make him/herself understood.	Pronunciation problems necessitate concentration on the part of the listener and occasionally lead to misunderstanding.	Always intelligible, although the listener is conscious of a definite accent and occasional inappropriate intonation patterns.	Pronunciation and intonation approximate that of a native speaker.
E. Grammar		Errors in grammar and word order so severe as to make speech virtually unintelligible.	Grammar and word order errors make comprehension difficult. Must often rephrase and/or restrict him/herself to basic patterns.	Makes frequent errors of grammar and word order that occasionally obscure meaning.	Occasionally makes grammatical and/or word order errors that do not obscure meaning.	Grammar and word order approximate that of a native speaker.

Figure 3 Student Oral Language Observation Matrix (The English Language Learner KnowledgeBase, 2004)

The first category on the matrix, Comprehension, refers to both speaking and listening comprehension because listening and speaking are intertwined. That is, you can't participate in a conversation if you don't understand what has been said.

Note that the matrix breaks the other aspects of oral language into four categories: fluency, vocabulary, pronunciation, and grammar. The descriptors for each of the categories are provided. The goal is to approximate a native speaker. Thus, students may score 5 on pronunciation without having mastered all of the phonemes. That's OK. Young native speakers haven't mastered them either. For more information on the phonemes which are difficult from a developmental standpoint, see Chapter 2 page 50.

Look at Extract 1. The teacher and the young learner are sitting together at a table. The teacher takes out a colorful picture of a family at the beach and prompts the child to talk about the picture. The teacher wants to determine specifically how well the child uses the present progressive tense (*be + ing*). The teacher carefully phrases her questions using the present progressive with the hope that the student responds using the target structure. As with all extracts in this book, T stands for *teacher* and S stands for *student*.

Extract 1

T: *Hi, Cindy. How are you today?*

S: *Fine.*

T: *Here are some pictures.*

S: *OK.*

T: *Let's look at the picture of the family at the beach. Do you like going to the beach?*

S: *Yeah.*

T: *Who do you see at the beach?* (The teacher points to the picture of the beach.)

S: *Mom, Dad, the brother, sister.*

T: *Can you tell me what that is?* (The teacher points to a blue picnic table and waits four seconds for response.)

S: *It is a desk blue.*

T: *It is a blue table.*

S: *Yeah, it is a blue table.*

T: *What is the mother doing?* (The teacher waits a full four seconds.)

S: *He is cutting the cake.*

T: (Smiles) *She is cutting the cake. What else is she doing?*

S: *Talking.*

The matrix in Figure 3 can help pinpoint the student's strengths and weaknesses even though the conversation isn't long enough to provide a thorough picture of Cindy's English. Cindy comprehended the questions very well. Her answers corresponded exactly with the questions. Cindy had trouble with some of the vocabulary. The fact that she mixed *desk* and *table* is not that unusual depending upon the types of desks in the classroom. She also made a grammatical error related to word order by putting the adjective after the noun rather than before it (*It is a desk blue*). However, Cindy was able to use the present progressive tense correctly.

From this conversation, the teacher not only determined Cindy was able to use the present progressive but also that Cindy was having some trouble with word order and pronouns. When you are teaching, you will want to set up situations where children will be required to use a specific grammatical construction. Remember, when you want to see how well children use a specific aspect of the language, you need to make sure that your question elicits the target construction.

Action

1. Look at the following list of questions and indicate which questions are good for assessing the past tense.

What was the weather like yesterday?	What did you do last night?
Did you go to the movies?	What did your teacher say?
What do you want to do this weekend?	Did you eat dinner?

2. Create a list of questions for assessing the future tense.

Share your answers with a classmate or colleague.

Assessing reading skills

Assessing students' literacy skills is a complex process (Hurley and Tinajero, 2001). It is especially difficult when students are learning ESL or EFL. In addition to assessing if students can decode, sound-out, or pronounce the words, you will also want to assess their ability to comprehend written text. Comprehension questions can be used to determine if children understand a specific reading passage.

Other techniques can also be used. One very effective technique is a **story map**–a graphic summary of a story. A story map can help you determine if students understand the main ideas of stories. Two of the most common story maps are the Story Elements Map and the Sequence of Events Story Map.

For a Story Elements Map, children are asked to describe the different parts–or elements–of a story. Specifically young learners are asked to describe the setting and characters. Learners can also be asked to describe the conflict and resolution. When using a Story Elements Map, tailor the descriptions of each section of the map to your students' language and literacy levels. In the reproducible Story Elements Map in Example 3, you will notice there are descriptors (setting, characters, conflict, and resolution) as well as questions. When using the map with students, you would choose which of these you would use. You would also decide if the children would write their answer in each section or draw pictures.

Example 3

Setting Place	**Characters**
Where does this story take place? The forest	*Who is in the story?* Hansel and Gretel
Conflict Problem	**Resolution**
What was the main or big problem in the story? Hansel and Gretel found an evil witch.	*What happened with the problem? How did the story work out?* A duck took them across the river so that they could go home.

A Sequence of Events Story Map chronicles what took place first, second, etc. It helps young learners focus on the most important events in the story. Like the Story Elements Map, children can write their responses or draw pictures to indicate what happened. Example 4 shows the key events of the story *Cinderella*. Note that some children might include the fact that Cinderella and the Prince live happily ever after. Other children would think that it was only necessary to mention that the Prince found Cinderella after the dance.

Example 4

Cinderella lived with a wicked stepmother.	Cinderella was invited to a fancy dance.	A fairy godmother helped Cinderella go to the dance.	Cinderella met a handsome prince.	Cinderella left at midnight and lost her shoe.	The prince found Cinderella using her shoe.

Action

Make a list of your favorite children's stories. Circle the name of a story you know very well. Create a Story Elements or Sequence of Events Story Map for the story that you circled.

Share your map with a classmate or colleague.

Writing assessment

Writing is assessed by eliciting and examining a sample of writing. The learners can write a sample consisting of a sentence, paragraph, or essay. This sample can be fiction or non-fiction and can be assessed using an analytic or a holistic rubric. Just as with speaking assessment, an analytic score is broken down into categories, and a holistic score is an overall score. However, the categories for an analytic writing assessment are slightly different from the categories that are used with an analytic speaking rubric.

The Northwest Regional Educational Laboratory developed an analytic rubric based on a total of seven traits which can be used with many different types of writing (Figure 4, pp. 154-155). Although the rubric was designed for elementary and secondary school students attending U.S. public schools and has been used extensively with ESL students in the U.S., it is also very useful for teachers teaching in an EFL setting. The rubric was designed to be used with both fiction and nonfiction pieces of writing.

Scoring 6+1 Trait™ Writing Assessment System

Ideas

The Ideas are the heart of the message, the content of the piece, the main theme, together with all the details that enrich and develop that theme. The ideas are strong when the message is clear, not garbled. The writer chooses details that are interesting, important, and informative—often the kinds of details the reader would not normally anticipate or predict. Successful writers do not tell readers things they already know; e.g., "It was a sunny day, and the sky was blue, the clouds were fluffy white …" They notice what others overlook, seek out the extraordinary, the unusual, the bits and pieces of life that others might not see.

Organization

Organization is the internal structure of a piece of writing, the thread of central meaning, the pattern, so long as it fits the central idea. Organizational structure can be based on comparison-contrast, deductive logic, point-by-point analysis, development of a central theme, chronological history of an event, or any of a dozen other identifiable patterns. When the organization is strong, the piece begins meaningfully and creates in the reader a sense of anticipation that is, ultimately, systematically fulfilled. Events proceed logically; information is given to the reader in the right doses at the right times so that the reader never loses interest. Connections are strong, which is another way of saying that bridges from one idea to the next hold up. The piece closes with a sense of resolution, tying up loose ends, bringing things to closure, answering important questions while still leaving the reader something to think about.

Voice

The Voice is the writer coming through the words, the sense that a real person is speaking to us and cares about the message. It is the heart and soul of the writing, the magic, the wit, the feeling, the life and breath. When the writer is engaged personally with the topic, he/she imparts a personal tone and flavor to the piece that is unmistakably his/hers alone. And it is that individual something—different from the mark of all other writers—that we call voice.

Word Choice

Word Choice is the use of rich, colorful, precise language that communicates not just in a functional way, but in a way that moves and enlightens the reader. In good descriptive writing, strong word choice clarifies and expands ideas. In persuasive writing, careful word choice moves the reader to a new vision of things. Strong word choice is characterized

Figure 4

(continued)

not so much by an exceptional vocabulary that impresses the reader, but more by the skill to use everyday words well.

Sentence Fluency

Sentence Fluency is the rhythm and flow of the language, the sound of word patterns, the way in which the writing plays to the ear, not just to the eye. How does it sound when read aloud? That's the test. Fluent writing has cadence, power, rhythm, and movement. It is free of awkward word patterns that slow the reader's progress. Sentences vary in length and style, and are so well crafted that the reader moves through the piece with ease.

Conventions

Conventions are the mechanical correctness of the piece–spelling, grammar and usage, paragraphing (indenting at the appropriate spots), use of capitals, and punctuation. Writing that is strong in conventions has been proofread and edited with care. Handwriting and neatness are not part of this trait. Since this trait has so many pieces to it, it's almost a holistic trait within an analytic system. As you assess a piece for convention, ask yourself: "How much work would a copy editor need to do to prepare the piece for publication?" This will keep all of the elements in conventions equally in play. Conventions is the only trait where we make specific grade level accommodations.

Presentation

Presentation combines both visual and verbal elements. It is the way we "exhibit" our message on paper. Even if our ideas, words, and sentences are vivid, precise, and well constructed, the piece will not be inviting to read unless the guidelines of presentation are present. Think about examples of text and presentation in your environment. Which signs and billboards attract your attention? Why do you reach for one CD over another? All great writers are aware of the necessity of presentation, particularly technical writers who must include graphs, maps, and visual instructions along with their text.

Figure 4 Scoring 6+1 Trait® Writing Assessment System (Northwest Regional Education Laboratory, 2001)

Portfolio assessment

A student portfolio is a collection of his or her individual work. Portfolios can help you see how individual children grow and develop over time (Gronlund and Engel, 2001). For the portfolio, the teacher and/or learner selects samples of classroom work that illustrate what has been done in class. A portfolio is intended to showcase a learner's development over time.

Portfolio assessment documents what a student can do. Portfolios can also be used to help children document for themselves what they know and can do.

There are many different types of items that can be placed in a portfolio. These include examples of student writing, activity sheets, audio recordings of the student speaking or reading orally, and projects. When using a portfolio, be sure to date each item. It is often useful to teach your students how to select items for their portfolio.

The Centre for Information on Language Teaching and Research (CiLT) has portfolio guidelines for children learning second or foreign languages (Figure 5). According to the guidelines, some of the portfolio pieces are self-assessments and are designed to help learners document what they are able to do with languages. Teachers are able to use this information as part of their overall assessment. As you can see, CiLT provides very specific guidelines which are both child-centered and teacher-friendly.

Getting Better! Self-assessment

What I can do in:

writing

	Approx. NC level single aspects	Approx. CoE level
I can copy single words without making mistakes.	1	A1
I can label pictures using words I know.	1	A1
I can copy phrases and sentences correctly.	2	A1
I have reached the equivalent of the Council of Europe's BREAKTHROUGH LEVEL in Writing		
I can write two or three sentences with help from my books.	3	A2
I can write about things I like and dislike.	3	A2
I can write some words and simple phrases from memory fairly well.	3	A2
I can write single sentences from memory and take notes for myself and others.	3–4	A2
I can write postcards and short messages to friends and family.	4	A2
I have reached the equivalent of the Council of Europe's WAYSTAGE LEVEL in Writing		
I can write a simple personal letter about myself and what I have been doing or what I am going to do.	5	A2–B1

Other

Figure 5 CiLt *My Language Portfolio: Teacher's Guide* (2004, p.11)

Portfolio assessment can be a wonderful way to gather information about individual children and groups of children. However, there are also disadvantages to portfolio assessment. Look at Figure 6 for some of the advantages and disadvantages to portfolio assessment.

Portfolio Assessment	
Advantages of Using Portfolios	Disadvantages of Using Portfolios
• Can be used for students at all stages of language development • Can reflect what students are learning and doing in class on a regular basis • Can show a young learner's progress over time • Can be used with virtually any coursebook	• Can be hard to figure out what should be included and who decides • Can be very easy to include too much • Can be difficult to evaluate the individual items • Can take a long time to learn how to use portfolios • Can take a long time to maintain and assess all your learners' portfolios • Can be difficult to assign grades to portfolios because the process is often more subjective than objective

Figure 6 Advantages and disadvantages of using portfolios

6. Assessment in the classroom

Assessing listening comprehension

The purpose of this section is to show you the concepts and techniques discussed in the chapter. Children's coursebooks often have one or two assessment pages at the end of each unit. The focus is often on listening since it is easier to assess **receptive skills** (listening/reading) than **productive skills** (speaking/writing) when dealing with groups of learners.

1. Look at the following page from *Hip Hip Hooray!,* a coursebook designed for 9- or 10-year-old children with some English-language literacy skills.

Hip Hip Hooray! 3 (Eisele, Hanlon, Eisele, and Hanlon, 2004, p. 56).

2. What are some questions that you could ask to assess a child's listening comprehension?

3. Why do you think this is or is not a good page for assessing listening? Consider what aspects of listening are being assessed?

4. Do students need to have English-language literacy skills to do this page? Why or why not?

Share your answers with a classmate or colleague.

Assessing speaking skills

Some coursebook pages can easily be used to assess young learners' speaking skills on an individual basis. Example 5 is a page from *Kinder Steps*. It is designed for four-year-olds without any English-language literacy skills.

Kinder Steps (Salvador and Gamboa, 2004, p. 122)

In Extract 2, the teacher starts the conversation by referring to the picture in Example 5. She is very careful to be positive. She starts by having the child respond nonverbally before she asks for a verbal response. She uses the picture as a starting off point for a conversation about how the child likes to play outside. The teacher is assessing if the learner could use the present continuous as well the present tense. The teacher is able to ascertain that her student could use both constructions correctly in a conversation format.

> ### Extract 2
>
> **T:** *Look at picture. Who do you see in the picture?*
> **S:** *Boys.*
> **T:** *Good. What are they doing?*
> **S:** *Playing.*
> **T:** (Points to the girl with the jump rope.) *What is she doing?*
> **S:** *Jumping.*
> **T:** *Yes, that's right. Where are they?*
> **S:** *Outside.*
> **T:** *Good. Do you like to play outside?*
> **S:** *Yeah.*
> **T:** *What do you like to play outside?*
> **S:** *To run and jump.*

Portfolio assessment

The portfolio items in Example 6 demonstrate a child's sense of her own speaking skills. Extract 3 (page 162) is an example of an exchange between a teacher and a student. Look at page 8 from the student portfolio.

CiLT *My Languages Portfolio* (2001, page 8)

T: *Please count from one to ten.*

S: *1, 2, 3, 4, 5, 6, 7, 8, 9, 10.*

T: *Very good. You counted one to ten. You can color in this bubble.*
(Points to the correct speech bubble.)

Action

Create examples of language use that demonstrate five other tasks in Example 6. Be sure to note which ones relate to the acquisition of English-language literacy skills.

Share your examples with a classmate or colleague.

7. Conclusion

Assessment is becoming more and more prominent in both ESL and EFL programs. As a teacher, it is something that you will be called to do on a continual basis. The purpose of this chapter was to explore language assessment as it relates to young learners. Issues impacting assessment were discussed. Strategies and techniques for assessing listening, speaking, reading, and writing were presented as well as portfolios as part of an overall program.

Further readings

Gronlund, G. and B. Engel. 2001. *Focused Portfolios: A Complete Assessment for the Young Child.* St. Paul, MN: Red Leaf Press, A Division of Resources for Child Caring.

This invaluable resource provides information on how to create portfolios. Information on collecting, maintaining, and sharing the results of portfolio assessment is provided in detail.

O'Malley, M. and L. Valdez-Pierce. 1996. *Authentic Assessment for English Language Learners: Practical Approaches for Teachers.* Reading, MA: Addison-Wesley.

This comprehensive guidebook provides teachers of school-age learners with practical advice on how to design a program that utilizes authentic assessment. It includes numerous checklists and rubrics.

Helpful Web sites

Cambridge Young Learners English Language Tests (www.cambridgeesol.org/exams/yle.htm)

This site provides information on the Cambridge Young Learners Exam. Several hundred thousand young learners between the ages of seven and 12 have taken the Cambridge Young Learners Exam.

Council of Europe: European Language Portfolio (www.coe.int/portfolio)

This site provides very useful information about putting together portfolios to assess language development. Links are constantly being added so it is helpful to check back often.

Northwest Regional Lab Analytic Writing Assessment (www.nwrel.org/assessment/index.php)

The Northwest Regional Educational Lab has developed a set of rubrics using analytic writing assessment. These rubrics were originally designed for native English speakers, but educators quickly discovered that they are also appropriate for use with children learning English as both a second and foreign language. These rubrics can easily be downloaded.

References

Brindley, G. 2003. Classroom-Based Assessment. In D. Nunan (ed.), *Practical English Language Teaching.* New York, NY: McGraw-Hill, 309-328.

Cameron, L. 2001. *Teaching Languages to Young Learners.* Cambridge, UK: Cambridge University Press.

Centre for Information on Language Teaching and Research (CiLT). *My Languages Portfolio* [updated 2001; cited 11 May 2005]. Available from http://www.nacell.org.uk/resources/pub_cilt/portfolio.pdf.

Centre for Information on Language Teaching and Research (CiLT). *My Languages Portfolio: Teacher's Guide.* [updated 2004; cited 11 May 2005]. Available from http://www.nacell.org.uk/resources/pub_cilt/teachers_revised.pdf

Daniels, H. and M. Bizar. 2004. *Teaching the Best Practice Way: Methods that Matter K-12.* Portland, ME: Stenhouse Publishers.

Eisele, B., R. Hanlon, C. Eisele, and S. Hanlon. 2004. *Hip Hip Hooray! 3.* White Plains, NY: Pearson Education, Longman.

The English Language Learner KnowledgeBase. *Student Oral Language Observation Matrix (SOLOM).* [updated 2004; cited 12 May 2005]. Available from http://www.helpforschools.com/ELLKBase/index.shtml.

Freeman D. and Y. Freeman. 2004. *Essential Linguistics.* Portsmouth, NH: Heinemann.

Georgiou-Ioannou, S. and P. Pavlou. 2003. *Assessing Young Learners.* Oxford, UK: Oxford University Press.

Gronlund, G. and B. Engel. 2001. *Focused Portfolios: A Complete Assessment for the Young Child.* St. Paul, MN: Red Leaf Press, A Division of Resources for Child Caring.

Hughes, A. 1989. *Testing for Language Teachers.* Cambridge, UK: Cambridge University Press.

Hurley, S.R. and J. V. Tinajero. 2001. *Literacy Assessment of Second Language Learners.* Needham Heights, MA: Allyn and Bacon.

Northwest Regional Education Laboratory. *6+1 Trait® Writing–Scoring.* [updated 11 January 2005; cited 11 May 2005]. Available from http://www.nwrel.org/assessment/definitions.php?d=1.

O'Malley, M. and L. Valdez-Pierce. 1996. *Authentic Assessment for English Language Learners: Practical Approaches for Teachers.* Reading, MA: Addison-Wesley.

Salvador, R.W. and F.C. Gamboa. 2004. *Kinder Steps: New Edition.* Mexico City, Mexico: Santillana Publishers, Richmond.

Chapter **Eight**

Working with parents of young learners

1. Introduction

In this chapter we will discuss why having a good relationship with your learners' parents is important. We will then move on to ways you can connect to your students' parents. Then I will layout a three-part plan: learning about the families of your learners, learning from the parents, and working with parents to support children's learning and development. This chapter also presents some of the challenges specific to working in **ESL** or **EFL** programs with parents.

2. Why are parents important?

When I first started teaching, I was armed with the latest methods for working with five-year-olds learning English as a foreign language. I had spent my university graduation money on books, toys, and games to equip my classroom. However, I was sorely lacking in the strategies and approaches necessary to effectively work with parents. I didn't realize that, although parents are not physically present in the classroom, they can and do judge teachers. Parents share their impressions, regardless of how valid they might be, with other parents, teachers, administrators, and members of the community. Moreover, when parents don't agree with or respect a teacher, they share their negative impressions with their children which can cause serious problems. For these reasons and many more, it is important to have a positive relationship with parents.

Parents support and are behind their children.

Educators have long recognized the importance and benefits of parental involvement in the education of children (Levinson, 1999). In fact as early as the late 19th century, schools in the United States offered advice to parents in the form of pamphlets (McCaleb, 1997). The need for schools to communicate with children's parents remains in place today. Schools and teachers should be compelled to create positive collaborations with learners' families (Lightfoot, 1978). Parental involvement in schools can help children develop socially, emotionally, cognitively, and academically. For the purpose of this chapter, the term *parent* is used even though it is recognized that many different family members may be **caregivers** for children such as grandparents or older siblings.

Some parents are more involved than others. Parents have a tendency to become less directly involved with their children's education as their children age (Eccles and Harold, 1996). Depending upon the cultural background of your students, you can expect parents of 12-year-olds to be less present than those of younger learners. If you are teaching in a culture different from your own, it is necessary to find out how involved parents tend to be in their children's education.

In the best circumstances, parents and teachers work together and create partnerships to help children develop socially and emotionally. For instance, think of a five-year-old child suffering from **separation anxiety**, fear of leaving her parent behind. When she starts kindergarten, the wise parent and the teacher work together to gently ease the distraught girl into the classroom.

Parents and teachers can also work together to help a child develop academically, especially if the child is having minor difficulties. Consider the nine-year-old boy who mixes up certain Russian Cyrillic letters with the English-language alphabet. Together the teacher and parent devise a plan. Each day at school, the teacher gives the boy a little extra English-language letter recognition instruction. Both the parent and son sit down every night after dinner and play a flash card game with English-language letters.

3. Ways that parents can be involved and connected

There are a wide range of ways that parents can be directly involved in their children's schooling. Some parents may drop their children off at the classroom door and be there to pick them up as soon as the bell rings. More often than not, these parents are avidly watching what goes on as they wait for their child. Other parents may attend regularly scheduled events such as the school opening ceremony, back-to-school night, assemblies, pageants, field trips, parent-teacher conferences, and parent-teacher meetings. In any endeavor with parents, communication is the key.

I believe that all teachers working with young learners should strive to help parents be both involved with and connected to their children's schooling. It is easier to make this connection if you share the same culture and speak the same language as the parents of your learners. However, even if you do not speak their language, you can still reach out to make the connections. Specific strategies for working with parents when you do not speak their language are included throughout this chapter.

Parent-Teacher Associations and Parent-Teacher Organizations

In a number of countries, there are **parent-teacher associations (PTA)** and **parent-teacher organizations (PTO)** where parents, teachers, and often administrators such as principals work together to improve the educational experiences for young learners. In some cases, PTAs focus on extracurricular activities such as field trips and class parties. In other situations, PTOs are more directly involved in curricular decisions. Teachers and parents may work together to select coursebooks or they may decide to add instrumental music to the curriculum for 11-year-olds.

Indirect parental involvement

There are also indirect ways that parents can be connected with the school. Parents who read every piece of written correspondence and visit the school's Web site are linked to their child's school through information. When parents march off to the store armed with the school supply list, they are working with the school to make sure that the child has the everyday tools necessary to be successful in the classroom. Parents who help children with their schoolwork and review their children's report cards are also linked to their child's school.

Parents as customers

Parents who pay for their children to attend private schools or institutes have a special link to the educational establishment by paying tuition. Although it may sound harsh, parents are customers when they send their children to private institutions. It is the parents, not the child, who pay for the school or institute. The parents have made a conscious decision to financially invest in their child's education. Often a specific school or institute has been chosen because it offers English. Parents can very easily withdraw their child if they are not satisfied with what they perceive is going on in the classroom.

1. Think about when you were a child. What types of contact did your parents have with your school? Did your parents take you to school every day, or did you get there on your own? Were there regularly scheduled events? What were these events? How were your parents involved in your education?

2. If you are a parent of a school-age learner, what types of contact do you have with your child's school?

Share your answers with a classmate or colleague.

Concerns about parental involvement and communication

Many teachers are wary of parents becoming too involved in schools. Teachers know that parents can be the sternest critics regarding the education of their children. They fear that given half the chance, parents will try to run the school. On occasion parents can be overbearing and unreasonable. However, generally speaking, if parents are treated with respect, they are usually more than willing to work with teachers. It is important to establish two-way communication early on. Parents can be your greatest ally and a real source of support.

When you don't speak the parents' language

You may find yourself in a situation where you do not speak the same language as the parents of your learners. Ideally, the school administration should work with you to make sure that there is someone who can provide oral interpretation and written translation services. It should be pointed out to your administrator that happy parents can be the real key to young-learner program success.

The person who provides translation services should be available to translate written notes that you may receive from your learners' families as well as notes that you may send. This individual should also be able to translate for parent-teacher conferences and when emergencies arise such as when a child becomes ill and needs to go home. It is also important that this individual be compensated for the interpretation and translation services that they provide. They shouldn't be expected to translate in addition to a full teaching schedule.

Some schools set up team teaching situations between teachers who are fluent in the child's home language and English-language teachers who do not speak the language of the child's home. Usually there is time for both teachers to get together and plan lessons. There should also be time set aside for the team to communicate together with the children's parents.

In case of emergency, you can also elicit help from an educator who is fluent in your student's native language in exchange for a service you can provide. For instance, you might offer to prepare art materials for a colleague who provides oral interpretation services. Try not to use children as translators since it can undermine a parent's role and authority.

4. Creating a teacher-parent partnership

Creating a partnership between parents and the school should be an ongoing process. In order to create a teacher-parent partnership, I follow a three-step plan that is the focus of this section. First, I take the time to learn about my learners' families. Second, I learn about what kind of children and learners my students are from their parents. It is important for teachers to remember that parents are experts regarding their own children. Finally, I work with the parents to create an educational partnership built on two-way communication and trust. By developing a partnership with parents, I am able to share the joy when my learners succeed.

Learning about your learners' families

The more that I know about a child's family, the better I am able to understand the individual learner and provide care and instruction tailored to meet their needs and circumstances. For example, I have had children in my classes whose mothers have not lived with them. By knowing this in advance, I am able to lessen their pain when valentines are made or Mother's Day is celebrated. If I know about the child's family, I can understand the context when children talk, draw, or write about situations that happen at home. I can also use carefully planned oral- and written-language activities to learn about children's home life.

In the English-language classroom, children often talk about their families because it is a common theme in children's English-language coursebooks. I also like to know who provides care for individual children. This helps me personalize the lessons by asking appropriate questions and giving appropriate suggestions. For instance, if an older brother appears frequently in Dae's drawings and writings, I might ask Dae questions about his brother when we are discussing families. For example, *What is your brother's name? How old is your brother?* or *What does your brother like to eat?*

If a child consistently draws her grandmother, I might suggest that she invite her grandmother to attend an assembly where she is going to perform. It doesn't matter if the grandmother speaks English or not, she will still get a thrill watching her granddaughter perform.

Children's drawings

One of the easiest ways to find out about your learners' home life is to pay attention to their drawings. You can give your learners **prompts** or suggestions that help you understand who cares for the child at home. Figure 1 provides a variety of drawing prompts which will give you insight into your students' home life. Drawing prompts do not necessarily have to come out of the blue. You can easily select a specific drawing prompt based on the English-language topic that your learners are currently studying. For example, if you are talking about food, you can give them the prompts dealing with food and dinner time.

Getting Ready for School Who gets you ready for school in the morning? Draw a picture of yourself getting ready for school. Who helps you or reminds you to get ready?	**Feeling Better** Have you ever been sick? Draw a picture of yourself at home when you were sick and a picture of yourself getting better. Who helped you feel better?
Food Who prepares your favorite foods for you? Draw a picture of the person who gets food ready for you. Draw a picture of them preparing the food.	**Dinner Time** Who do you eat dinner with? Draw a picture of yourself eating dinner at home. Be sure to draw pictures of the people who you eat with.
Getting Ready for Bed Who gets you ready for bed at night? Draw a picture of yourself getting ready for bed. Who helps you or reminds you to get ready?	**Story Time** Who tells you stories? Draw a picture of yourself listening to a story being told or read to you.

Figure 1 Drawing prompts

Reflection

Think back on your own childhood. Look at the drawing prompts in Figure 1. If you were a child and you had been asked to draw a picture based on the prompt for feeling better what would you have drawn? Who would have been in your pictures? What would have been going on in the pictures?

Share your answers with a classmate or colleague.

Children's writings

Children with literacy skills can write answers to questions about their home life. There are a variety of different writing activities that you can have children do which will help you to become more knowledgeable of your students' home life. The writing activities that you select and the way you present them will depend upon their literacy level in English and the amount of writing that you expect learners to do as part of your program. For example, children can complete sentences such as the one provided in Chapter 1 (page 20), *I like to have _____ help me when it is hard for me to do something.* Figure 2 has four more writing suggestions for writing prompts for older, higher-level students.

Scared	**Reminders**
If you woke up in the middle of the night and were scared, who would come and help you feel better? Write a conversation between yourself and the person who would make you feel better.	Who reminds you to do different things such as your homework or to go to bed? Write a conversation between yourself and the person who reminds you to do different things.
Good News	**Rules for a Martian**
Make a list of the really good things that could happen to you. For instance, you could get a perfect grade on your reading test. Your team could win a race. Pretend that something really good has happened. Who would you tell? Write a conversation between yourself and the person who you would like to tell.	Pretend that you are writing a letter to someone from Mars who is going to visit your home. The Martian has no idea how to act or behave on Earth. What advice would you give to the Martian? What would you tell the Martian to do?

Figure 2 Writing prompts

Action

Think back to when you were a child. If something wonderful had happened, who would have been the first person, besides a friend your own age, whom you would have told? With a classmate or colleague, create a conversation between an adult and a child sharing good news. Use the example below as a model. *Note that this is translated from Spanish.*

Grandmother: Hi, Lupita.
Lupita: Hey Grandma, you won't believe it.
Grandmother: Take off your backpack and come and sit down.

Lupita:	Remember the mask I was making? The one for the role-play in English class.
Grandmother:	Yes, you didn't want to go to bed last night 'cause you were too busy finishing it up.
Lupita:	Oh yeah. The teacher said it was the best mask she has ever seen. She even took me in to see Mrs. Braddock, the principal, and she showed it to her.
Grandmother:	I am so proud of you.

Share your conversation with a different classmate or colleague.

Learning from parents

Parents have a great deal of knowledge regarding their own children. You should tap their expertise even though it may be difficult to do so if you do not speak their language. There are a variety of ways to gain information from parents. Parents can fill out questionnaires at the beginning of the school year that the administration will hopefully translate into English as needed. Parents can also share information through interview-style conferences at the beginning of the school year. The types of questions that can be asked as well as how you can use what you learn from parents are given in Figure 3.

Sample Questions	Using the Information in Your Classroom
What does your child like to do in her free time?	If the child is interested in soccer, you can try to include books, in English, about soccer in the classroom reading corner.
Does your child prefer playing alone or with other children?	If the child prefers playing alone, you might give her opportunities to work alone and not always in a pair or group.
What language(s) has your child been exposed to? What languages are spoken in your home? Has your child ever been to a country where English is the dominant language? Does your child enjoy watching films or reading books in English?	If the child has had additional exposure to the English language, then you may want to make sure that the child is consistently challenged.

Figure 3

(continued)

Does your child have any hearing problems or has your child had chronic ear infections?	If the child has had hearing problems, then you will want to make sure that you modify your instruction to meet the needs of a child who is hearing impaired. (See page 23 for more information on addressing the needs of children with hearing impairment.)

Figure 3 Information from parents

Open-ended letters

In some schools, parents are asked to write a letter about their child in the family's home language. When necessary, the school administration can assist in the translation of these letters into English. In these letters, parents are invited to provide the teacher with any useful insights regarding the child as both a person and a learner. Parents are free to write a few lines or a few pages. At first you might think that the parents will only praise their children. In fact, parents are usually very honest about their children. It is not uncommon for a parent to write things such as, "Kailai is a very smart little girl. However, she can be so lazy. She would prefer to look out the window than to finish her work." Or "Tonyo was born prematurely and he has been trying to catch up ever since. Although he is smart, physically he is not very well coordinated. I understand he is chosen last to be on the soccer team."

Reflection

1. Think about your own childhood. If your parents had been asked to write a letter to one of your teachers, what would they have said?

2. If you have a school-age child, what would you tell your child's teacher?

Share your answers with a classmate or colleague.

Weekend reports

In one private kindergarten I know of, every Monday morning the parents send a short report describing what the family did over the weekend. This type of information makes it easier for the teachers to personalize their lessons.

The parents fill out a form (Figure 4) in their native language and send it in with their child. (If you don't speak the child's native language, you may want to pre-arrange to have someone translate the notes into English.)

Child's Name: _____ **Date:** _____

What did your family do over the weekend? Did you go any place special? Did you have a special celebration such as a family birthday? Did anyone visit your house? Who came to visit?

_____

_____

_____

Figure 4 Weekend report

In Extract 1, the teacher uses the information from the form to ask guided questions, in English, about what the child has done. The teacher is careful to insert the vocabulary that the child needs to answer the question. For example, the child gives an answer that doesn't exactly match the question. The teacher goes on and asks another question that has the answer embedded within the question. The teacher is able to do this because of the information provided by the parents. The teacher is also able to **personalize** a lesson about zoo animals for this individual child. As with all the extracts in this book, T stands for *teacher* and S stands for *student*.

> **Extract 1**
>
> **T:** *Where did you go over the weekend?*
> **S:** *It was fun.*
> **T:** *Did you go to the zoo or the movies?*
> **S:** *The zoo.*
> **T:** *What did you see?*
> **S:** *Animals.*

1. Make a list of the different types of activities that children do with their families during the weekend. These can include going to the movies, cooking, reading books, and having friends over.

2. Find a partner and create a dialogue between a teacher and a child. Use Extract 1 as a model.

Share your answers with a classmate or colleague.

Working with parents

There are many ways that you will interact with parents on a regular basis. You should strive to create a cooperative atmosphere where you work together to help children achieve their potential. Good communication requires a great deal of effort and is the key to satisfied parents who will be able to team with you to help children do their very best. You will need to share information with parents and also to elicit help and information from them on a regular basis. If you do not speak the same languages as your learners' parents, then you will probably need to elicit assistance from someone who speaks their language and English. There are some parents who may be able to communicate with you in English.

Listed below are suggestions that will help you to create and maintain a positive relationship with parents. Relationships take time to evolve and this is definitely the case between teachers and parents.

Program information

It is important to share information about your English-language program with parents because it will help them to better comprehend what goes on in their children's classrooms. Some parents feel very strongly that children must learn English the same way that they themselves learned English. However, ideas on how to teach English have changed significantly over the past 20 years. Therefore, when some parents believe that a real English class must focus on grammar or it is not academic enough to do any good, part of your responsibility will be explaining how art activities, music activities, and story-telling help children develop their English communication skills. The information can be shared in the form of newsletters, Web pages, and/or parent informational meetings.

Be sure to give parents an opportunity to voice their questions and concerns regarding the English-language program. If you hold an information session, include adequate time for parents to ask questions. If you post program information on a Web page, be sure to provide an email address where parents can send you questions and comments.

Homework

Homework is one way, albeit often indirectly, that parents are involved with their children's school. Homework is a charged issue and something worth discussing with parents. Homework is a very complex and little researched topic that impacts students, teachers, and parents and that has many dimensions including cultural ones (Hong and Milgram, 2000). Parents from some cultures complain if children do not receive what they believe is to be a sufficient amount of homework, whereas members of other cultures do not want their children overburdened with schoolwork.

How involved parents are with their child's homework varies tremendously. Some parents may sit and help their child while others will expect their children to remember to do their homework and to do it independently. And yes, there are some unsavory parents who do their children's homework for them.

Homework is an especially tricky issue for English-language teachers. Parents may not speak English and may feel frustrated or worried that they will lose face if they can't understand their child's homework. Other parents may look at their child's homework and come to the conclusion that their child is spending too much time learning informal expressions rather than focusing on the formal ones that they had to memorize as a child.

There are a few rules that I follow when assigning homework. I always make sure that the homework clearly reflects the program goals that I have shared with parents. I let parents know what nights of the week that they should expect homework as well as how long it should take children to do it. I always make sure that homework is a review of the content that has been covered in class, and I make sure that my students know how to do it. Instead of home-work, "home-fun" can be assigned where children have do something enjoyable such as making props for a role-play.

Reflection

What types of homework activities did you have as a child? Did anyone at home help you with your homework? Who provided assistance? What kind of assistance did they provide? If you took a foreign language, did the person who helped you speak that language?

Share your answers with a classmate or colleague.

Report card comments

Giving report cards and grades is a common part of teaching. Report cards can be a good communication tool between teachers and parents. Teachers of young learners provide feedback to parents on how well the children are performing academically as well as how well they are behaving in class, getting along with others, and trying to do their best. Often you will be expected to write comments about individual children's overall performance. There should also be a space on report cards for parents to write comments back to the teacher.

One warning for a teacher: it can be a real challenge to make sure that your comments are tailored to the individual child and do not begin to sound alike at the end of the day. One technique some teachers use is to keep **anecdotal records**–observations of individual learners' accomplishments. Anecdotal records can be kept very easily with a set of index cards on a metal ring. You should have one index card for each child and one metal ring per class. When a child accomplishes something, write down the accomplishment and the date on the child's card. When it comes time to write report card comments or to have parent-teacher conferences you will have a set of specific remarks that you can use. Many of the remarks are related directly to young learners' English-language development.

Figure 5 is a nice starting point for report card comments that are not anecdotal records, but remember, you should try to personalize your comments as much as possible.

Finished Work

Assignments are not legible

Needs to be encouraged to check over work before turning it in

Is very careful with assignments

Improvement

Is learning how to listen

Is learning how to print neatly

Is learning how to write neatly

Is developing more confidence

Listening skills are improving

Speaking skills are improving

Reading skills are improving

Writing skills are improving

Is learning to help others

Language Specific Comments

Expresses creative ideas

Understands everything said in class

Has difficulty listening to English-language stories

Has listening skills appropriate for age/grade level

Has speaking skills appropriate for age/grade level

Has reading skills appropriate for age/grade level

Has writing skills appropriate for age/grade level

Listening skills could use improvement

Has good reading skills

Reading skills could use improvement

Is an avid reader

Does not seem to enjoy listening to stories or books being read aloud

Appears to enjoy listening to stories and books being read aloud

Does not seem to enjoy reading stories or books in English

Appears to enjoy reading stories and books in English

Seems reluctant to speak aloud for fear of making mistakes

Has excellent English-language pronunciation

Is a very creative writer

Figure 5

(continued)

English-language pronunciation could use improvement

Has a very good listening vocabulary

Has a very limited listening vocabulary

Has a very good speaking vocabulary

Has a very limited speaking vocabulary

Has a very good reading vocabulary

Has a very limited reading vocabulary

Has a very good writing vocabulary

Has a very limited writing vocabulary

Organization

Has well-organized supplies

Has trouble organizing her backpack

Has trouble organizing the supplies on her desk

Can never locate his supplies such as pencils and paper

Social/Emotional Development

Could spend more time listening to others

Bothers others (such as hitting or pushing)

Is very friendly towards others; He is always smiling

Gets upset very easily. Lacks self-control

Does not get upset easily; Has a lot of self-control

Interrupts others

Says things which are unkind

Makes an effort to say things which are kind

Has trouble staying in her seat

Is impatient and always trying to get attention

Is very patient

Lacks confidence

Is confident

Helps others when they are having difficulty

Is unaware of the needs of others

Is very aware of others' feelings and emotions

Is always willing to work with any other child in the class

Is only willing to work with one or two other children

Work Habits

Completes work on time

Has trouble staying on task for more than four or five minutes at a time

Pays attention to detail

Has trouble following instructions

Follows complex instructions

Has trouble focusing and concentrating

Could put forth more effort

Hard worker

Never completes work on time

Figure 5 Report card comments

Parent-teacher conferences

Some schools schedule parent-teacher conferences on a regular basis, while other schools have parent-teacher conferences only on an "as needed" basis. A parent-teacher conference can be a scheduled pre-arranged face-to-face meeting, or it can be an impromptu two-minute chat on the front steps of the school. It can also take place on the telephone or by email. Personally, I don't recommend communicating with parents by email because it isn't as personal and can be a very harsh way to communicate a concern you have about a child.

When you communicate with parents about their children's performance and behavior, be specific. Parents, just like their children, need specific feedback. Faint praise is not very useful. If you are having a face-to-face conference with a parent, you might want to pull out samples of the child's work. You may want to show a sample of what a child wrote at the beginning of the year and a sample of what the child wrote last week. Then take the time to show the parent areas of improvement with the child's writing.

A formula that many teachers follow is to first talk about a child's strengths and then move onto areas where improvement is needed. By starting with the strengths, parents realize that you see the child as a whole and not just as a problem or a set of problems. After mentioning areas where the learner could improve, you should always elicit the help and advice from parents. Try to make sure that you are having a dialogue with parents and not just a monologue where the parents are listening and you are talking.

Look at Extract 2. Note that the parent is very anxious and that the teacher tries to put her at ease. The teacher gives very specific feedback. The teacher also listens to the parent's suggestion and shows her eagerness to follow up on the parent's ideas. In the extract, P stands for *parent*.

Extract 2

T: *Thank you so much for coming today.*

P: *I will do whatever I can to help Yoko.*

T: *Yoko's written work is beautiful. Let me show you some of the things that she has done in the last week. You can see her drawing is very advanced for a seven-year-old. She writes beautifully for someone who has only been studying English for a year. Her thoughts and ideas are very well developed. Look at this story that she wrote about her stuffed dog, Wini.*

P: *Thank you.*

T: *I am a little bit concerned about Yoko.*

P: *What seems to be the problem? Has she done something wrong?*

T: *Oh, no, not all. There is a little problem, however. I think that is something that you might be able to help me with. You see Yoko is very shy about speaking in class. She always covers her mouth and whispers. I think that she is afraid that she is going to make a mistake or not pronounce something right.*

P: *My English is terrible, so I know just how she feels. I always hated being called on in class.*

T: *What could we do to make Yoko feel more comfortable?*

P: *She doesn't like sitting in the front of the class because she is afraid that everyone is watching her.*

T: *Well, I didn't realize that. I could easily move her to the back.*

P: *That would be good.*

T: *I was also wondering if I could send you questions home in advance. That way you could rehearse the answers with her so that she will get the right answer.*

P: *Would we need to do that forever?*

T: *No, probably just for a week or so to help her gain some confidence.*

1. Make a list of five types of problems that children may have in school. Be sure to include one or two problems that occur during recess or on the playground as well problems in the classroom.

2. Write a conversation between a parent and a teacher discussing two of the problems you listed above.

Share your conversation with a colleague or classmate.

There are also situations when teachers are frustrated and do not communicate as effectively as they could with parents. Sometimes they feel that they are being honest by being very direct. It is also very easy to convey one's frustration directly to a parent without being careful to use a manner and a language which is constructive.

1. Look at Extract 3, a telephone conversation between a parent and the teacher. The teacher has called the parent because Michael, an eight-year-old, has been hitting other children in class and speaking very rudely to her.

2. Work with your classmates or colleagues to create a more productive conversation between the parent and teacher.

Extract 3

P: *Hello.*

T: *Hello, Mrs. Karp, this is Mrs. Johnson, Michael's teacher.*

P: *Oh hello. How are you?*

T: *Fine. Thank you. Well, I am calling because I am very upset with Michael.*

P: *What's wrong?*

T: *He was just terrible today, in fact, he has been terrible all week. He has to be better in school.*

P: *I can't really blame him.*

T: *What do you mean?*

P: *You see his father and I are getting divorced. Michael's dad moved out last week.*

Weary children

Children are being pushed by their parents further and harder to acquire skills and knowledge at early ages (Rosenfeld and Wise, 2000). The march toward academic success begins for some children when they are infants and are placed into computer-based programs designed just for them (Elkind, 2001). As a teacher, you may be confronted with parents who are literally wearing their children out with extra classes. For example, it is not uncommon in some Asian countries, for young learners to have up to four hours of lessons after school plus homework. Often times, children are being bombarded with activities designed to help them become well-educated.

Parents often believe that young children should begin learning a foreign language while they are in preschool (Marinova-Todd, Marshall, and Snow, 2001). There is a wide-held belief that children learn languages better than individuals who are older (Nunan, 2003). Parents may fear and communicate a real sense of anxiety that if their children do not learn English at an early age, they will not be able to develop adequate English-language skills. There are advantages of learning a language earlier from the standpoint of pronunciation (Flege, 1999). However, there is great debate among professionals regarding the overall advantages and disadvantages of learning a language at an early age (Hyltenstam, Abrahamsson, 2001; Marinova-Todd, Marshall, and Snow, 2000, 2001).

If children are showing signs of weariness—such as falling asleep in class, being overly cranky, or excessively yawning—they may simply be tired and need more rest. If children cannot wake up on their own, they generally are not getting enough sleep. As a teacher, you may need to sit down with parents and discuss ways to make sure that children get enough rest. If parents are providing private lessons for their children, they need to be advised that children do not have to learn English when they are very young. Children's overall health is more important than learning English.

Do children in your country have too many activities or too many things to do? Make a schedule for a typical child between the ages of five and 12. If you do not know any children between these ages, think back to your childhood and write out a typical schedule. Are there too many structured activities? Is there enough time for play?

Share your answers with a classmate or colleague.

Working with families who have extra connections to the English language

It is more and more likely that you will have learners in your classes who have had extra exposure to the English language. There are many different situations and scenarios that give children extra contact with English outside of the classroom. A child may have a mother who is a native English speaker and a father whose native language is French. "Mixed language marriages are on the increase as international borders open and communications between countries become easier" (Baker, 2000, pg. xvii).

Consider a Russian boy living in Moscow whose parents speak Russian as their native languages. The father uses English exclusively at work and has decided to use that language as the only language to communicate with his son. There are also many children now accompanying their parents to English-speaking countries for short and long periods of time.

Parents are often stymied as to which language or languages they should be helping their children learn (Esch and Riley, 2003). This is a very private and personal decision and as a teacher, you should support parents regardless of their decision. It is something that parents need to think about within the context of their personal family situation, work situation, and their future plans.

As a teacher, it is up to you to work with family members to build upon any English-language skills that they have helped their children to develop. If children have skills which are above their peers because of outside linguistic exposure, they should be challenged in the classroom. You can work with parents to develop a classroom plan. For instance, a child who has learned to read in English might have a set of English books that she can read while the rest of the class is working on the development of beginning English-language literacy skills.

Language enrichment at home

Parents often ask me for ways that they can support their children's English-language development at home. I usually suggest that parents and children use English during a special family time when they are all together.

For instance, everyone in a family can sit down and watch a movie in English as a special family event. The movie can be a cartoon or nature program or anything else that has a lot of pictures and context. Music and tapes can be listened to in the car or on family music night. However, parents should be reminded of the importance of helping their children to develop language skills in their native language.

5. Conclusion

Parent involvement can often be perceived as a blessing or curse when working with young learners. In this chapter, I provided a brief overview of the reasons that you should develop a positive partnership with the parents of your young learners. I laid out a three-part plan for developing the partnership. First, learn about your young learners' families, next you learn from their parents, and finally, you work with parents to support children in their learning and overall development. I also touched upon some of the issues that you may encounter as you work with parents of learners developing English-language skills.

Further reading

Baker, C. 2000. *A Parents' and Teachers' Guide to Bilingualism, 2nd Edition.* Clevendon, UK: Multilingual Matters.

This book addresses the issues that parents raise when thinking about what language and languages to use with their children. It is especially appropriate for teachers who have children in their classes who come from mixed-language marriages.

Helpful Web sites

Parent Zone (http://www.parentzonescotland.gov.uk)

This is a site for both parents and guardians of school-age learners in Scotland. Although the information is specific to Scotland, the site can be a model for educators wishing to collaborate with parents.

The U.S. based Parent Teacher's Association (http://www.pta.org/)

This site is designed to help parents become more involved in their children's education. This site provides information about how the association serves as an advocate.

References

Baker, C. 2000. *A Parents' and Teachers' Guide to Bilingualism, 2nd ed.* Clevendon, UK: Multilingual Matters.

Eccles, J. and R. Harold. 1996. *Family Involvement in Children's and Adolescents' Schooling.* In Dunn, J. and A. Booth. Family-School Links: How Do They Effect Educational Outcomes? Mahwah, NJ: Lawrence Erlbaum.

Elkind, D. 2001. *The Hurried Child: Growing up Too Fast Too Soon, 3rd ed.* Cambridge, MA: Perseus.

Esch, E.H. and P. Riley. 1986, 2003 (first published 2003). *The Bilingual Family: A Handbook for Parents.* Cambridge, UK: Cambridge University Press.

Flege, J.E. 1999. *Age of Learning and Second Language Speech.* In Bird Song D. Second Language Acquisition and the Critical Period Hypothesis Mahwah. NJ: Lawrence Erlbaum.

Hong, E. and R. Milgram. 2000. *Homework: Motivation and Learning Preference.* Westport, CT: Bergin and Garvey.

Hyltenstam, K. and N. Abrahamsson. 2001. Age and L2 learning: The hazards of matching practical "implications" with theoretical "facts." *TESOL Quarterly.* 35: 151–170.

Levinson, M. 1999. *The Demands of Liberal Education.* Oxford, UK: Oxford University Press.

Lightfoot, S. L. 1978. *Worlds Apart: Relationships between Families and Schools.* New York, NY: Basic Books.

Marinova-Todd, S., D.B. Marshall, and C. Snow. 2000. Three misconceptions about age and L2 learning. *TESOL Quarterly.* 34: 9–34.

Marinova-Todd, S., D.B. Marshall, and C. Snow. 2001. Missing the point: A response to Hyltenstam and Abrahamsson. *TESOL Quarterly.* 35: 171–176.

McCaleb, S.P. 1997. *Building Communities of Learners: A Collaboration among Teachers, Students, Families, and Community.* Mahwah, NJ: Lawrence Erlbaum.

Nunan, D. 2003. The Impact of English as a Global Language on Educational Policies and Practices in the Asia-Pacific Region. *TESOL Quarterly.* 37: 589–613.

Rosenfeld, A. and N. Wise. 2000. *The Over Scheduled Child: Avoiding the Hyper Parenting Trap.* New York, New York: St. Martin's Press.

Chapter **Nine**

Key issues in teaching young learners

1. Introduction

In this final chapter, key issues related to teaching young learners are explored. While there are many issues we could discuss in this chapter, I have chosen to focus on ones teachers face on a regular basis. Teaching **ESL** or **EFL** to young learners is an evolving field, and many efforts are being made around the world to improve the process for both teachers and students.

In this chapter, you will read about ways to work with children and to effectively manage their behavior in the classroom. You will also become more aware of the special needs that learners have including different intelligences. You will also learn about working with children on a one-to-one basis as well as the dangers that children face when they work on the Internet.

2. Classroom management

One of the biggest challenges facing teachers of young learners is classroom management. On one hand, you want to be a kind and loving caregiver for your students. You don't want to be a taskmaster children fear. On the other hand, you want to maintain order in your classroom so that instruction can take place. Creating the balance between a caring environment and one where there is control is not an easy task for any teacher. However, it's especially difficult for new teachers. In this section, we will look at some classroom management strategies that will facilitate an environment that is conducive to learning.

Establish clear rules at the beginning of the year.

Children appreciate knowing what your expectations are. It's important to have rules that are stated in positive terms and establish what the children are expected to do clearly. At the beginning of the school year, and whenever you feel the students need to review the rules, demonstrate or point out expected behavior. For example, *Watch how I keep my hands to myself when I walk.* or *Look at how all of the children at this table are listening.*

There are a number of things you should do with the establishment of rules. First and foremost is to find out what your school's policies are regarding rules. Your supervisor should be able to tell you if a set of rules exist. There may also be a list of rules in the teacher's handbook. You also need to find out whether rules have been sent to parents in their native languages. These may or may not be exactly the same rules as in the teacher's handbooks because one set of rules may have been updated without the others also being updated. Whenever possible, the rules should be consistent among different teachers. The consequences for breaking the rules should also be consistent among the faculty and staff.

It is also important to communicate the rules to learners as well as their parents. The list of rules can be sent home to students in their native language. However, you shouldn't assume that the parents have taken the time to go over the rules with their children. Therefore, you should also read and explain the rules to your students. I personally like to demonstrate the rules in front of learners. The rules can also be posted in the classroom in English with hand-drawn pictures to illustrate them.

Look at the chart. Change the negatively stated rules to positively stated ones. The first one has been done for you.

Negative Rule	Positive Rule
Don't hit others.	Keep your hands to yourself.
Don't talk loudly.	
Don't push other kids.	
Don't eat in the classroom.	
Don't forget to bring your classroom supplies to class.	

Share your rules with a classmate or colleague.

Teach the concept of appropriate and inappropriate behavior.

The teacher is complimenting her students' appropriate behavior.

The terms *good behavior* and *bad behavior* are relative and can be problematic. When you tell children that they are being bad, they often internalize it that they are bad children and not that their behavior at that moment could be interpreted as bad. As a teacher of young learners, you need to monitor yourself to make sure you comment on the appropriateness of your learners' behavior and not on the children themselves. For your learners, it's important that you spend time discussing the concept of appropriate and inappropriate behavior. For example, you may want to teach children that it is inappropriate to shout or run in the classroom, whereas it can be very appropriate to shout and run with their friends outside on the playground.

Offer rewards judiciously.

Often teachers will give children rewards for good work. Unwittingly, by misusing rewards, teachers can contribute to an atmosphere of competition that is unhealthy (Paul, 2001). It is important to instill in your learners some sense of pride in their own accomplishments rather than a reliance on external gratification. Having said this, there are times when rewards are in order. If a child has gone from consistently not finishing her work during the allotted time to finishing it on time, then you might want to let her select a special sticker to attach to her paper.

Personally, I am concerned about the use of candy as a regular reward. Providing sweets for parties or special events is one thing, but doling out candy on a regular basis sends the wrong message. Besides candy not being good for children's teeth and contributing to obesity–a problem that unfortunately is becoming more pronounced in children in many parts of the world–giving candy as a reward teaches young learners that sugar and sweets can be used as a way to reward oneself. As an alternative to candy, you can give stickers or an extra five minutes of recess time.

Plan more than you think you will need.

Always be sure to have enough activities to keep children engaged, paying attention, or **on-task**. Nothing leads to chaos more quickly than children who don't have anything to do. You may want to prepare a set of back-up activities that you or a substitute teacher can use at a moment's notice. It is easier to *not* get to all your planned activities than to come up with an engaging task while a class full of fidgeting students is eagerly looking at you and asking, "What's next?"

Also, these tasks should not be photocopier dependent. You may be in a teaching situation where you think you can dash into the office before (or even during) class and make copies. Photocopiers break down at the most inopportune moments. It is useful to have a stash of activities planned that do not require you to run off pages for each learner. Look at Figure 1 (page 190). These are the types of activities that you may want to put aside in case of emergencies.

- Tried and true finger-plays and songs, including the audio-recording (A great resource is www.theteachersguide.com/ChildrensSongs.htm)
- Art activities which only require scissors, paper, crayons, and markers
- Games which can be played on the chalk or whiteboard (such as tic tac toe where children have to use a specific word in order to draw an *X* or an *O* on the board) Note, I personally feel that hangman is used far too much and only has limited educational value.
- Reading aloud two or three of your learners' favorite books
- A set of brain teasers appropriate for your learners' age and language levels (for older students, a good resource is http://hlavolamy.szm.sk/brainteasers/logic-puzzles.htm)
- Board games and other language-focused games (such as Scrabble for older children) which students can do at their seats

Figure 1 Back-up activities

Balance activities.

Most children do not have very long attention spans. Also, not every child is going to enjoy or learn from the same type of activities. In order to keep children engaged, you will want to include a balance of activities. By balanced I mean that you want some noisy activities and some quiet ones, some large-group activities mixed with some small-group or individual activities. Figure 2 is a list of balanced activities that would keep learners engaged during a 40-minute class period.

4–5 minutes	Warm up with finger-plays and songs
2–3 minutes	Discussion of weather, days of the week, announcements (whole group)
6–8 minutes	Story (whole group)
13–15 minutes	Art activity: as a follow-up to the story (individual)
4–6 minutes	Discussion of different things made by children during the art activity (This can be done in small groups or the whole class.)
6–8 minutes	Writing activities (small groups)
1–2 minutes	Clean up (individuals and small groups)
4–5 minutes	Wind down with finger-plays and songs (whole group)

Figure 2 Example of balanced activities

Action

You are teaching the story *Goldilocks and the Three Bears* (pages 34–35) to a class of seven-year-olds using the balanced activities outlined in Figure 2. Write a detailed lesson plan about what you would do for each activity.

Share your lesson plan with a classmate or colleague.

Provide specific feedback.

Correcting behavior and providing feedback is an important part of your job as a teacher of young learners. The type of feedback you give children should be specific and related to what they are doing. For instance, if a child is looking out the window and not paying attention, you will want to say *Charlene, you have been looking out the window for about five minutes. Instead you need to look at your paper so that you can get your work done.* or *I really like the way the children at this table are sitting. Everyone is looking at the board and waiting patiently for the next set of instructions.*

When you have given feedback and the misbehavior continues, there are a number of different recourses at your disposal. You can separate the child from the rest of the learners or send the child to the office for a time-out. However, you have to be careful to never embarrass or shame the child who is misbehaving. Talk to other teachers who are also working or have worked with the child to find out what they have tried in the past. Finally, you can talk to the parents or schedule a meeting between the parents, the school administrator, and yourself to discuss the situation and possible remedies.

Action

1. Make a list of three positive and three negative behaviors that occur in a classroom with six-year-old children; for example, learners who are paying attention.

2. Now take each behavior and describe it using very specific language. For example, *I notice that three children are looking carefully at the board while I am writing.* In order for children to know that it is appropriate behavior I might add, *I am very pleased.*

Share your answers with a classmate or colleague.

Know when to use the child's native language.

When I did my student teaching, a supervising teacher was very adamant that I should not use the children's native language with them, even though both the students and I spoke Spanish. She was upset one day when she walked in and heard me speaking Spanish to them. I pointed out that there had been tears on the playground and it seemed more appropriate to be a caregiver at that moment rather than a teacher. In emergency situations, it is appropriate to use the child's native language or to find someone who is able to communicate with the child in her native language.

However, while teaching, I try to use only English because I feel it makes me a better teacher. By staying in English, I am forced to deliver better instructions, and I will often use more varied types of input instead of always giving spoken instructions. For example, I may pantomime the instructions or draw pictures on the board of what I want students to do.

Unfortunately, that only takes care of part of the question. The other part is what should be done when children start using their native language? This will happen and often children unwittingly drift into their native language when they are excited about a game or other activity. When it does happen, I will say to the children, *This is an English language game.* or *This is an English book.* I prefer to do this for two reasons. First, I am not demeaning the children's native language by saying they should not speak it. Second, they also become aware that the game or the book is what dictates the use of English. This way, I can also easily remind learners about specific phrases they need to use in order to play the game or talk about the book in English.

Finally, when children are entering or leaving the classroom and naturally talking to one another in their native language, I do not stop them—especially in an EFL setting where English is not their main form of communication.

3. Special needs

Many learners in classrooms have special needs that require some sort of intervention. These needs range from visual and hearing impairments to other specific problems which will impact learning. In recent years, more attention has been paid to the special educational needs of learners who are bilingual and/or attempting to learn an additional language (Baca and Cervantes, 1998; Winzer and Mazurek, 1998). On a personal note, I am especially interested in special needs as they relate to ESL and EFL students because my father was a second-language learner in the U.S. and also completely blind in one eye. Even with these special needs, he learned the strategies necessary to tackle complex academic material and graduated from Stanford University at the top of his class.

Teachers of young learners are more likely to encounter special needs in the classroom than teachers of older learners for two reasons. First, the vast majority of children in the world—unless they have severe disabilities—attend school. Unfortunately, older learners with learning disabilities may have dropped out of school. Second, young learners with special needs may not yet have developed or been taught the strategies necessary to tackle academic subjects.

Therefore, you may be the first person they encounter who can help them learn these strategies.

While children with severe special needs will probably not be in your class without their own caregiver, you may have a child who is visually or hearing impaired. (Signs of vision impairment are found on page 74 and hearing impairment on page 23.) In addition, you may have students who have **dyslexia** or an **attention deficit disorder**. As a teacher, not a medical professional, you cannot and should not even attempt to make a diagnosis of either of these conditions. However, you can tell the appropriate educators at your school if you sense that a learner may have a special educational need. Once a diagnosis is made, you can work with a specialist to develop a repertoire of strategies that can be used to help the learners with the special needs.

Dyslexia

Dyslexia is a learning disability that impacts children learning their native language as well as learning EFL or ESL. One of the most famous people to suffer from dyslexia is the actor Tom Cruise. Historically referred to as word-blindness, the term *dyslexia* is based on the Greek language meaning *difficulty with words*. The cause of dyslexia is not known but there are known links to heredity and to early hearing loss. There is both mild and severe dyslexia. For example, a student with dyslexia may confuse left and right. It should be noted that if a child is left-handed, that in and of itself is not related to dyslexia. Another example of dyslexic behavior may be a student who is able to read a word in one paragraph, but when the word appears in a subsequent paragraph, the student is at a complete loss.

Regardless of the degree of dyslexia, early diagnosis of the problem and focused instruction are key. EFL teachers may find it inappropriate to provide learners with English-language literacy instruction until they have mastered literacy skills in their native language. If, for example, a child is having trouble mastering symbols—such as letters or characters in his own language—it doesn't make sense to load him with an additional set of symbols before the original ones have been mastered.

Unfortunately, many EFL teachers may find themselves in a country where most primary school teachers have had little formal training to effectively meet the needs of dyslexic learners. Or they may feel that there are no resources available to help learners who may be dyslexic. If this happens to you, chances are once you start talking to teachers who specialize in teaching reading to young learners, you will find someone or a group of people who are aware of dyslexia and may even have resources to help.

Figure 3, taken from the British Dyslexia Association's Web site (see page 202 for the address) is a list of indications teachers pay attention to.

If a child has several of these indications, further investigation should be made. The child may be dyslexic or there may be other reasons. This is not a checklist.

1. Persisting factors

There are many persisting factors in dyslexia, which can appear from an early age. They will still be noticeable when the dyslexic child leaves school.

These include:

- Obvious 'good' and 'bad' days, for no apparent reason
- Confusion between directional words, e.g. up/down, in/out
- Difficulty with sequence, e.g. with days of the week or numbers
- A family history of dyslexia/reading difficulties

2. Pre-school (5 and under)

- Has persistent jumbled phrases, e.g. "cobbler's club" for "toddler's club"
- Use of substitute words e.g. "lampshade" for "lamppost"
- Inability to remember the label for known objects, e.g. "table, chair"
- Difficulty learning nursery rhymes and rhyming words, e.g. "cat, mat, sat"
- Later than expected speech development

Pre-school non-language indicators

- May have walked early but did not crawl—was a "bottom shuffler" or "tummy wriggler"
- Persistent difficulties in getting dressed efficiently and putting shoes on the correct feet
- Enjoys being read to but shows no interest in letters or words
- Is often accused of not listening or paying attention
- Excessive tripping, bumping into things, and falling over
- Difficulty with catching, kicking, or throwing a ball, hopping and/or skipping
- Difficulty with clapping a simple rhythm

3. Primary school age (5 years old to 12 years old)

- Has particular difficulty with reading and spelling
- Puts letters and figures the wrong way round
- Has difficulty remembering tables, alphabet, formulae, etc.
- Leaves letters out of words or puts them in the wrong order

Figure 3

(continued)

- Still occasionally confuses *b* and *d* and words such as *no/on*
- Still needs to use fingers or marks on paper to make simple calculations
- Poor concentration
- Has problems understanding what he/she has read
- Takes longer than average to do written work
- Problems processing language at speed

Primary school age non-language indicators

- Has difficulty with tying shoelaces, tie, dressing
- Has difficulty telling left from right, order of days of the week, months of the year, etc.
- Surprises you because in other ways he/she is bright and alert
- Has a poor sense of direction and still confuses left and right
- Lacks confidence and has a poor self-image

Figure 3 Indications of dyslexia (British Dyslexia Association, 2005)

Attention Deficit Disorder/Attention Deficit Hyperactivity Disorder

When I ask groups of experienced teachers of young learners if they have ever had a child with **Attention Deficit Disorder (ADD)** or **Attention Deficit Hyperactivity Disorder (ADHD)**, they instantly nod their heads. Even though teachers cannot and should not diagnose children with this disorder, you may recognize a number of signs and symptoms. You need to report any situation where you see a child displaying numerous indicators of ADD or ADHD.

If a child is diagnosed with ADD or ADHD, you need to work with the specialist provided by the school to develop a plan to meet the child's needs, yet at the same time, you do not want to disrupt the rest of your learners. Figure 4 will help you recognize signs and symptoms of ADD and ADHD as well as become familiar with strategies to help the learners in your classroom.

Signs and Symptoms of ADHD and ADD

- Fails to give close attention to details or makes careless mistakes
- May have poorly formed letters or words or messy writing

Figure 4

(continued)

- Has difficulty sustaining attention in tasks or play activities
- Does not follow through on instructions and fails to finish schoolwork or chores
- Avoids or strongly dislikes tasks (such as schoolwork) that require sustained mental effort
- Forgetful in daily activities
- Has difficulty organizing tasks and activities
- Loses things necessary for tasks or activities (pencils, assignments, tools)
- Shows difficulty engaging in leisure activities quietly
- Acts as if "driven by a motor" and cannot remain still
- Blurts out answers to questions before the questions have been completed, often interrupts others

Strategies for Children with ADHD and ADD

- Allow a child to change work sites frequently while completing homework or studying
- Assign tasks involving movement such as passing out papers, running errands, watering plants
- Use music as a tool for transitioning from one activity to another
- Vary tone of voice: loud, soft, whisper
- Stage assignments and divide work into smaller chunks with frequent breaks
- Teach students to verbalize a plan before solving problems or undertaking a task
- Permit a child to do something with hands while engaged in sustained listening: stress ball, worry stone, paper folding, clay
- Use inconspicuous methods such as a physical cue to signal a child when she or he tunes out
- Provide opportunities for student to show divergent, creative, imaginary thinking and get peer recognition for creativity
- Employ multi-sensory strategies when directions are given and lessons presented

Figure 4 Signs and symptoms of ADHD and ADD; strategies for working with children with ADHD or ADD (Adapted from Learning Disabilities Association of America, 2005)

There are many children who are disorganized. For some children, it is a sign of a learning disability, whereas for others, it is a personality characteristic. What would you do to help a child whose learning supplies and materials are always in disarray? At what point would you want to talk to the parents or school's administrator about the child's disorganization?

Share your answers with a classmate or colleague.

4. Multiple intelligences

For many years now, Howard Gardner of the Harvard Graduate School of Education has drawn attention to the different ways that people can be smart (Gardner, 1985). He has identified seven original areas of intelligence: mathematical-logical, inter-personal (understanding others), intra-personal (understanding one's self), bodily kinesthetic, verbal linguistic, musical, and spatial. Subsequently, an additional intelligence, naturalist (ability to discern patterns in nature), has been added to the core list.

Gardner's theory of multiple intelligences is very important for teachers working with young learners because it provides a framework for looking at children's strengths. It is very sad if a child is saddled with a laundry list of all of the things that she can't do before she even has a full set of teeth. With Multiple Intelligence theory, teachers can look at and build upon learners' strengths.

Teachers tend to teach to their own preferred intelligences (Nicholson-Nelson, 1998). You will want to include activities in your day-to-day lesson planning that stretch each child to excel and feel success. For instance, you may want to include a logic puzzle with geometric shapes for students who have logical-mathematical intelligences. For intrapersonal students, you might create learning stations where they can work alone. For children with verbal intelligence, you might want to make sure that they have sufficient time to spend at the writing center. For bodily kinesthetic learners, you might want to have them dance to English-language songs. For students with verbal linguistic intelligence, you might want to provide them with extra English-language books to read or give them word puzzles to do. For students with interpersonal intelligence, you may want to include activities which require them to work with partners or in small groups. For students with naturalist intelligence, you may want to include science books about nature.

Choose one activity from Chapter 2, 3, or 4 and state how you would adapt the activity for each type of intelligence.

Share your answer with a classmate or colleague.

5. Tutoring

You may be in a situation where you are giving private English-language lessons to children on a one-to-one basis. In many ways, teachers find tutoring more difficult than working with several children for a variety of reasons. First, you have to provide constant energy and attention which isn't necessary when children are together and can get some of this from each other. Second, parents may have unrealistic expectations about the amount of material that can be covered in a session. Third, children may be referred to tutoring because they are having trouble in school. They may have special needs which have not been diagnosed, or if they have been diagnosed, adequate recommendations for how to address them have not been provided.

It is important to have realistic expectations regarding what can be covered and learned in a tutoring session and in a series of tutoring sessions. From the beginning, you need to sit down with the parents and negotiate what the expectations are from your perspective as well as from theirs. For example, you may find yourself explaining to parents that you can not *make* a child, who has never spoken English, fluent in six months.

You should also match the activities to the language cognitive level and intelligences of the learner. Select activities and content based on the learner's interests. This may mean extra time planning your lessons since your learner's interests may be unique. For example, you may find yourself searching online for the English names for horseback riding equipment. Finally, observe how much the student is able to absorb during a session as well as the learner's interest level during each activity.

Just as it is important to have a plan for a class full of students, it is also necessary to plan when you are teaching students on a one-to-one basis. If you were asked to tutor a nine-year-old for the first time, what information would you want to have in advance?

Outline the language background, age, and gender of a young learner. Then make a list of questions you would want answered before your first tutoring lesson. Finally, create a lesson plan for the first hour-long lesson.

Share your answers with a colleague or classmate.

6. Technology

The expansion, or rather explosion, of the Internet has been invaluable for teachers of young learners. If you are living and working in a country where there is limited access to English-language materials, then you are probably delighted at all of the resources that you can now access via the Internet. For example, throughout this book, I have provided numerous Web sites that can help you become a better equipped teacher. If you do have Internet access, I would strongly advise you to spend a couple of hours a month searching the Web for new information on teaching young learners.

The teacher is supervising his students when they are on the Internet.

While the Internet can be a useful tool to use with your learners, safe sojourning on the Internet is an issue that should be taken into account when setting up technology-based programs for young learners (Lewis, 2004). Before you allow children in your classes to use the Internet, be sure that you have the skills and expertise to properly supervise them. You would not allow young learners to explore the neighborhood around your school without adequate supervision. The same amount of caution must hold true for the Internet. Without adequate supervision, children can easily become victims to Internet crime and can visit sites which are very inappropriate for them. Before allowing students to use computers in your classroom, at the very least make sure you know how to set and use the parental blocks.

In addition, it is very easy for anyone, especially children, to accidentally download a computer virus. Following all of the safeguards for computing is difficult enough for an adult, let alone for a young learner. It is important to use a strong firewall and virus protection program and to perform virus scans on a regular basis.

Reflection

Which Helpful Web sites mentioned in this book have you visited? Which ones did you find to be the most useful? Why? If you haven't visited any of the Web sites, which ones would you like to visit? Why?

7. Professional support

As was mentioned previously in this chapter, teaching English to young learners is an evolving field. Traditionally, teachers were either trained as English-language specialists or as specialists in the education of young children. Very often, these two teacher education programs did not even exist in the same higher education institution. Because of this, it has and is taking longer for the specialty of teaching ESL or EFL to young learners to evolve. I would recommend that anyone teaching young learners ESL or EFL to join a professional organizer aimed at helping teachers work with EFL and ESL learners.

Two of the most well-known professional organizations designed to support teachers working with students who are learning English as a second, foreign, or additional language are Teachers of English to Speakers of Other Languages (TESOL) and International Association of Teachers of English as a Foreign Language (IATEFL). TESOL has done a great deal of work to advance the profession of teaching ESL to young learners in the United States. Their efforts for teaching EFL to young learners have not been quite as comprehensive. IATEFL, on the other hand, is focused on EFL and in recent years has been putting more and more emphasis on young learners. Both organizations have affiliates in many different parts of the world and have Web sites (see page 202).

In addition, there is another professional organization aimed at helping teachers of school-age learners. The Association of Supervision and Curriculum Development (ASCD), which has affiliates in many parts of the world, is aimed at helping teachers. On a daily basis, ASCD sends out SmartBriefs via email. SmartBriefs is a summary of articles on interesting educational developments from around the world.

8. Conclusion

In this chapter, I presented a number of different issues that impact teachers working with young learners. I discussed classroom management because it is necessary to create an optimum environment so that learning can take place. Next, I discussed special needs because many children do have special educational needs which should be addressed so that learners can maximize their potential. In the same vein, multiple intelligences were discussed because this theory helps teachers look for the strengths within each child. I also talked about tutoring and the use of the Internet because these may very easily impact your work in the young-learner classroom. Finally, I suggested several professional organizations that teachers of young learners can join for extra support and information.

 Further readings

Murray, B.P. 2002. *The New Teacher's Complete Sourcebook. Grades K–4.* New York, NY: Scholastic Professional Books.

This book provides highly effective suggestions for both setting up and managing a classroom. Although it is aimed at new teachers, the information is also valuable for veteran teachers.

Nicholson-Nelson, K. 1998. *Developing Students; Multiple Intelligences.* New York, NY: Scholastic Professional Books.

This book offers invaluable information for teachers wanting to address learners' different intelligences in the classroom. This book focuses on activities which not only cater to learners' different intelligences but also help learners develop higher-order thinking skills.

 Helpful Web sites

ASCD SmartBrief (www.smartbrief.com/ascd/index.jsp)

This is the location to sign up for free SmartBriefs described on page 200.

The Association for Supervision and Curriculum Development (ASCD) (www.ascd.org)

This non-profit professional organization with more than 170,000 members advocates the best possible educational practices for all learners. ASCD has affiliates in many different parts of the world.

The British Dyslexia Association (www.bda-dyslexia.org.uk)

This site calls itself "the voice of dyslexic" people. It is a non-profit organization that provides basic information on dyslexia as well as links to a number of different sites. Although the information is aimed at people in the United Kingdom, it does have links to worldwide organizations designed to help individuals with dyslexia.

Education World (www.educationworld.com)

This site provides a wide variety of resources for teachers working with school-age learners. In order to access quick activities, look under lesson planning and five-minute fillers.

International Association of Teachers of English as a Foreign Language (IATELF) (www.iatefl.org)

This professional organization is aimed at helping teachers working in non-English speaking settings. It has a very active interest section for teachers working with young learners.

Learning Disability Association of America (http://www.ldanatl.org)

This nonprofit association with members throughout the United States and 27 other countries serves as an advocacy organization for individuals with learning disabilities. This site provides a wealth of information about learning disabilities.

Walter McKenzie's Multiple Intelligence Pages (http://surfaquarium.com/mi)

This site provides useful information about the different intelligences.

Teachers of English to Speakers of Other Languages (www.tesol.org)

This professional organization based in the United States is aimed at helping teachers working with students learning English in both English and non-English speaking countries.

References

Baca, L.M. and H.T. Cervantes. 1998. *The Bilingual Special Education Interface.* Upper Saddle River, NJ: Merrill-Prentice Hall.

British Dyslexia Association. *Indications of Dyslexia.* [updated 2 March 2004; cited 6 May 2005]. Available from http://www.bda-dyslexia.org.uk/extra320.html.

Gardner, H. 1985. *Frames of Mind.* New York, NY: Basic Books.

Learning Disabilities Association of America. *Attention Deficit Disorder/Attention Deficit Hyperactivity Disorder (ADD/ADHD).* [updated 2 March 2004; cited 6 May 2005]. Available from http://www.ldanatl.org/aboutld/teachers/understanding/adhd.asp.

Lewis, G. 2004. *The Internet and Young Learners: Resource Books for Teachers of Young Students.* Oxford, UK: Oxford University Press.

Murray, B.P. 2002. *The New Teacher's Complete Sourcebook. Grades K–4.* New York, NY: Scholastic Professional Books.

Nicholson-Nelson, K. 1998. *Developing Students; Multiple Intelligences.* New York, NY: Scholastic Professional Books.

Paul, D. 2003. *Teaching English to Children in Asia.* Hong Kong, PRC: Longman Asia ELT.

Winzer, M. and K. Mazurek. 1998. *Special Education in Multicultural Contexts.* Upper Saddle River, NJ: Merrill-Prentice Hall.

Appendix

Children's songs and finger-plays

THE ALPHABET SONG

A-B-C-D-E-F-G, H-I-J-K-L-M-N-O-P,
Q-R-S, T-U-V, W-X, Y-Z,
Now I know my A-B-C's,
Tell me what you think of me?

BINGO

There was a farmer had a dog
And Bingo was his name-o.
B-I-N-G-O, B-I-N-G-O,
B-I-N-G-O, and Bingo was his name-o.
… *(clap)* –I-N-G-O
… *(clap)-(clap)*-N-G-O
… *(clap)-(clap)-(clap)* –G-O
… *(clap)-(clap)-(clap)-(clap)* –O
… *(clap)-(clap)-(clap)-(clap)-(clap)*

BUMBLEBEE

Bumblebee was in the barn,
(circle finger in air)
Carrying his dinner under his arm.
(circle finger closer to child)
Bzzzzzz……….

CLAP YOUR HANDS

Clap, clap, clap your hands
As slowly as you can.
Clap, clap, clap your hands
As quickly as you can.
Shake, shake, shake your hands
As slowly as you can.
Shake, shake, shake your hands
As quickly as you can.
Roll, roll, roll your hands
As slowly as you can.
Roll, roll, roll your hands
As quickly as you can.
Rub, rub, rub your hands
As slowly as you can.
Rub, rub, rub your hands
As quickly as you can.
Wiggle your fingers
As slowly as you can.
Wiggle your fingers
As quickly as you can.
Pound your fists
As slowly as you can.
Pound your fists
As quickly as you can.

FIVE LITTLE FISHIES

Five little fishies swimming in a pool,
First one said, "The pool is cool."
Second one said, "The pool is deep."
Third one said, "I want to sleep."
Fourth one said, "Let's dive and dip."
Fifth one said, "I spy a ship."
Fisherman's boat comes,
Line goes ker-splash,
Away the five little fishies dash.

GRANDMA'S GLASSES

Here are Grandma's glasses,
(fingers around the eyes)
Here is Grandma's hat,
(hands on head)
This is the way she folds her hands,
(fold hands)
And lays them in her lap.
(folded hands in lap)
Here are Grandma's glasses,
(larger glasses)
Here is Grandpa's hat,
(larger hat)
This is the way he folds his arms,
(fold arms across chest)
Just like that.
(with emphasis)

HEAD AND SHOULDERS

(Point to each body part as they are mentioned)
Head and shoulders, knees and toes, knees and toes,
Head and shoulders, knees and toes, knees and toes
Eyes and ears and mouth – and – nose,
Head and shoulders, knees and toes, knees and toes.

HICKORY DICKORY DOCK

Hickory Dickory dock, the mouse ran up the clock.
The clock struck one, the mouse ran down,
Hickory, Dickory dock.

HUMPTY DUMPTY

Humpty Dumpty sat on a wall,
Humpty Dumpty had a great fall;
All the king's horses and all the king's men
Couldn't put Humpty together again.

HUSH, LITTLE BABY

Hush little baby, don't say a word,
Papa's going to buy you a mockingbird.
If that mockingbird don't sing,
Papa's going to buy you a diamond ring.
If that diamond ring turns brass,
Papa's going to buy you a looking glass.
If that looking glass gets broke,
Papa's going to buy you a billy goat.
If that billy goat don't pull,
Papa's going to buy you a cart and bull.
If that cart and bull turn over,
Papa's going to buy you a dog named Rover.
If that dog named Rover don't bark,
Papa's going to buy you a horse and cart.
If that horse and cart fall down,
You'll still be the sweetest little baby in town.

IF YOU'RE HAPPY

(Clap when the statement is true.)
If you're happy and you know it, clap your hands.
If you're happy and you know it, clap your hands.
If you're happy and you know it, then your face will
  surely show it.
If you're happy and you know it, clap your hands.
If you're happy and you know it, stomp your feet.
If you're happy and you know it, stomp your feet.
If you're happy and you know it, then your face will
  surely show it.
If you're happy and you know it, stomp your feet.
If you're happy and you know it, shout hurray.
If you're happy and you know it, shout hurray.
If you're happy and you know it, then your face will
  surely show it.
If you're happy and you know it, shout hurray.
If you're happy and you know it, clap your hands,
  stomp your feet, shout hurray.
If you're happy and you know it, clap your hands,
  stomp your feet, shout hurray.
If you're happy and you know it, then your face will
  surely show it.
If you're happy and you know it, clap your hands,
  stomp your feet, shout hurray.

IT'S RAINING

It's raining, it's pouring,
The old man is snoaring.
He went to bed and bumped his head
And couldn't get up in the morning.

JACK AND JILL

Jack and Jill went up the hill, to fetch a pail of water;
Jack fell down and broke his crown,
And Jill came tumbling after.
Up Jack got and home did trot
As fast as he could caper,
Went to bed to mend his head
With vinegar and brown paper.
Jill came in and she did grin
To see his paper plaster,
Mother, vexed, did scold her next,
For causing Jack's disaster.

LONDON BRIDGE

London Bridge is falling down, falling down, falling
  down,
London Bridge is falling down, my fair lady.
Build it up with iron bars, iron bars, iron bars,
Build it up with iron bars, iron bars, iron bars, my
  fair lady.
Build it up with gold and silver, gold and silver, gold
  and silver,
Build it up with gold and silver, my fair lady.
Take the key and lock her up, lock her up, lock her
  up,
Take the key and lock her up, my fair lady.

THE MULBERRY BUSH

Here we go around the mulberry bush,
The mulberry bush, the mulberry bush,
Here we go around the mulberry bush,
So early in the morning.
This is the way we wash our face,
Wash our face, wash our face,
This is the way we wash our face,
So early in the morning.
This is the way we comb our hair,
Comb our hair, comb our hair,
This is the way we comb our hair,
So early in the morning.
This is the way we brush our teeth,
Brush our teeth, brush our teeth,
This is the way we brush our teeth
So early in the morning.
This the way we put on our clothes,
Put on our clothes, put on put clothes,
This is the way we put on our clothes,
So early in the morning.

MOTHER'S KNIVES AND FORKS

These are mother's knives and forks,
(fingers interlaced, tips up)
This is mother's table,
(flatten hands and arms)
This is Mother's looking glass,
(palms toward face)
And this is baby's cradle.
(palms up, rock arms)

OH WHERE, OH WHERE HAS MY LITTLE DOG GONE?

Oh where, oh where has my little dog gone?
Oh where, oh where can he be? With his ears
Cut short and his tail cut long, Oh where, oh where
Can he be?

OLD MACDONALD HAD A FARM

Old Macdonald had a farm, E-I-E-I-O!
And on his farm he had some chicks, E-I-E-I-O!
With a chick, chick, here and a chick, chick there,
Here a chick, there a chick, Everywhere a chick,
   chick,
Old Macdonald had a farm, E-I-E-I-O!
And on his farm he had some ducks, E-I-E-I-O.
With a quack, quack here and a quack, quack there,
Here a quack, there a quack, everywhere a quack,
   quack,
Chick, chick here, and a chick, chick there,
Here a chick, there a chick, everywhere a chick,
   chick,
Old Macdonald had a farm, E-I-E-I-O.
And on his farm he had a cow, E-I-E-I-O.
With a moo, moo here and a moo, moo there,
Here a moo, there a moo, everywhere a moo, moo,
With a quack, quack here and a quack, quack there,
Here a quack, there a quack, everywhere a quack,
   quack,
Chick, chick here, and a chick, chick there,
Here a chick, there a chick, everywhere a chick,
   chick,
Old Macdonald had a farm, E-I-E-I-O.
And on his farm he had a turkey, E-I-E-I-O.
With a gobble, gobble here and a gobble, gobble
   there,
Here a gobble, there a gobble, everywhere a gobble,
   gobble,
With a moo, moo here and a moo, moo there,
Here a moo, there a moo, everywhere a moo, moo,
With a quack, quack here and a quack, quack there,
Here a quack, there a quack, everywhere a quack,
   quack,
Chick, chick here, and a chick, chick there,
Here a chick, there a chick, everywhere a chick,
   chick,
Old Macdonald had a farm, E-I-E-I-O.
And on his farm he had a pig, E-I-E-I-O.

With an oink, oink here, and an oink, oink there,
Here an oink, there an oink, everywhere an oink,
With a gobble, gobble here and a gobble, gobble
   there,
Here a gobble, there a gobble, everywhere a gobble,
   gobble,
With a moo, moo here and a moo, moo there,
Here a moo, there a moo, everywhere a moo, moo,
With a quack, quack here and a quack, quack there,
Here a quack, there a quack, everywhere a quack,
   quack,
Chick, chick here, and a chick, chick there,
Here a chick, there a chick, everywhere a chick,
   chick,
Old Macdonald had a farm, E-I-E-I-O.
And on his farm he had a donkey, E-I-E-I-O.
With a hee-haw here, and a hee-haw there,
Here a hee-haw, there a hee-haw, everywhere a hee-
   haw,
With an oink, oink here, and an oink, oink there,
Here an oink, there an oink, everywhere an oink,
With a gobble, gobble here and a gobble, gobble
   there,
Here a gobble, there a gobble, everywhere a gobble,
   gobble,
With a moo, moo here and a moo, moo there,
Here a moo, there a moo, everywhere a moo, moo,
With a quack, quack here and a quack, quack there,
Here a quack, there a quack, everywhere a quack,
   quack,
Chick, chick here, and a chick, chick there,
Here a chick, there a chick, everywhere a chick,
   chick,
Old Macdonald had a farm, E-I-E-I-O.

Glossary

alphabetic language – a language that is written using an alphabet

analytic rubric – individual or separate scores within a rubric; for example, if you were grading written papers, you could have one individual score for mechanics and another for organization

anecdotal records – observations that teachers make of individual learner's achievements and accomplishments

articulate – to produce a clear or specific utterance

assessment – gathering information and using that information to create opinions on the learner's progress

attention deficit disorder (ADD) / attention deficity hyperactivity disorder (ADHD) – the main characteristics are inattention and inability to stay on task

audiolingual method (ALM) – a language teaching method based on the notion that learning another language is a matter of acquiring new linguistic habits through drill and practice

auditory – pertaining to sound

brainstorm – a prewriting strategy involving generating as many ideas, words, or concepts related to a given topic as possible

caregiver – someone who provides care to children—can be a parent, brother, sister, grandparent, other relative, teacher, etc.

choral response – a technique where learners respond in unison

cognitive development – intellectual development

cognitive skills – the skills used for remembering, reasoning, understanding, problem solving, evaluating, and using judgment

Communicative Language Teaching (CLT) – a language teaching approach based on the concept that interaction is the key to language learning and that students must have opportunities to communicate during lessons

comprehensible input – input that is slightly above a learner's knowledge level and yet understandable for the learner

configuration – shape made up of letters within a word

context – the situation in which language occurs

context clues – clues that help a learner to better comprehend or understand a text

decode – sounding out words

deep processing – working with information at a high cognitive and/or personal level which will make it more likely that the information will be remembered

developmentally appropriate practices, instruction, interaction – tasks with children that are tailored to the individual child's development

direct instruction – formal presentation of concepts, vocabulary items, etc.

dyslexia – difficulty with words; impacts a learner's ability to read, write, and spell

emergent literacy – when a variety of reading skills merge often as a result of young learners figuring out the process on their own

emotional development – an affective aspect of development related to feelings

error correction – the process of correcting learners' errors

evaluation – the collection and interpretation of information which can be used for making decisions

finger-plays – simple chants and rhymes recited with accompanying hand or finger motions

fishbowl – a technique where the teacher models the small group or pair work activity with another learner or learners while the rest of the class looks on

fluency – the ability to speak or write fluidly and confidently and at a rate that is consistent with children of the same age

genre – a specific kind of written composition

graphic organizers – tools used to visually organize information

high-frequency words – that occur over and over again

holistic/holistic scoring – based on a single score for student performance; is frequently used in large-holistic rubric-scale assessments of writing skills

indirect instruction – instruction based on a learner discovering content with indirect assistance from the teacher

innovations – when children create their own verses and versions of existing songs, finger-plays, and stories

language acquisition – usually refers to the more natural way that a child learns his or her native language with focus being on communication

language experience approach – learners participate in an experience, dictate the experience back to their teacher, and then use the written dictation as material for reading

language learning – usually refers to the type of language instruction that takes place in a classroom with focus being on form

learning channels – the preferred ways that learners receive and process information

lexical – relating to words and vocabulary

listening capacity – an informal measure of one's ability to understand or comprehend spoken language in the context of a story being told or read aloud

literature-based approach – reading skills that are taught using authentic literature

mean length of utterances – based on the mean number of morphemes found within a sample of utterances

minimal pair – two words with the only variation between them being one phoneme

morpheme – the smallest meaning unit in language

on task – refers to a child who is engaged in an activity such as singing a song with the group, listening as a teacher reads a story, or doing a worksheet

overgeneralization – to apply a rule, such as a grammar rule, and "overuse" it in situations where it does not apply

Parent-Teacher Associations (PTA)/Parent-Teacher Organizations (PTO) – organizations designed to help parents and teachers work together on behalf of children

personalize – to link the lesson directly to a learner's personal experience

phoneme – speech sound that can be put together with other speech sounds to make words

phonemic awareness – the awareness of different sounds that make up words

phonics – sound-letter correspondence

phonics-based instruction – instruction with phonics as the focus

phonological awareness – the ability to listen and think about the entire range of sounds that occur in a word

physical development – the development of fine (small) and gross (large) motor skills

portfolio – a collection of a learner's work

pre-teach – teach in advance, such as in pre-teaching vocabulary before students read or are exposed to a written passage

process writing – teaching approach that places importance on different aspects of the cycle of writing, including invention, drafting, and revision, and not just the final product produced

productive – producing language, as in speaking and writing

prompt – a question or picture designed to prompt young learners to write or talk about a specific topic

publishing – the step involved with finishing a piece of writing so that it is ready to be shared

readiness skills – skills that prepare children to do other skills; for example, reading readiness skills get children ready to read

receptive – receiving language, as in listening and reading

reliability – consistency of test results for a specific group of learners over time

role-play – playing different roles or acting out different parts

rubric – a scale used for assessment

scaffolding – a type of support tailored to meet a child's needs and abilities; it is designed to help a child gain skills and to become autonomous

separation anxiety – greater than normal concern and anxiety about leaving one's parent or guardian

sight words – words that can be read on sight without having to decode each letter

social development – the skills necessary to have positive relationships with others

story map – a visual or graphic summary of a story

tactile – pertaining to touch or feel

Total Physical Response (TPR) – a teaching method in which language learners respond physically to commands or descriptions given in the target language

utterance – things that people say

validity – when a test measures what it is designed to measure

visual – the images that one sees

wait time – the amount of time that a teacher waits for a response

Zone of Proximal Development (ZPD) – the distance between what a child can do alone or independently and what the child can do with some support

Index

Abrahamsson, N., 182
ADD/ADHD (Attention Deficit
    Disorder/Attention Deficit
    Hyperactivity Disorder), 195–196
ALM (Audiolingual Method),
    52–55
alphabetic languages, 69
analytic rubrics, 148–151
Anderson, N., 71
anecdotal records, 178
appropriateness, 188–189
articulation, 50
ASCD (Association of Supervision
    and Curriculum Development),
    200
Asher, James J., 30
Ashton-Warner, Sylvia, 85–86
assessment, 138–164
    classroom-based overview, 145
    coursebook activities, 157–162
    of development, 6–12
    elements of, 138–140
    and expectations, 141
    formal, 143–145
    instructions for, 142
    of listening, 146–148, 157–158
    portfolio, 10, 155–157, 161–162
    of reading, 151–153
    and report cards, 178–179
    of speaking, 148–151, 159–160
    and trust, 143
    and wait time, 141
    of writing, 153–155
Association of Supervision and
    Curriculum Development
    (ASCD), 200
Attention Deficit Disorder/
    Attention Deficit Hyperactivity
    Disorder (ADD/ADHD),
    195–196
Audiolingual Method (ALM),
    52–55
auditory learners, 25–27. See also
    learning channels
auditory patterns, 29
    and listening, 35, 38
    See also repetition

Baca, L. M., 192
back-up activities, 189–190
Bailey, K., 60
Baker, C., 183
balance of activities, 190–191
Beck, I., 122, 124
bedtime stories, 72
beginning consonant sounds, 79–80
Bergeron, B. S., 78

Berk, L. E., 14
Berril, D. P., 102
Birdsong, D., 49
Bizar, M., 139
Blachowicz, C. L., 126
Boyle, O. F., 69, 70, 77, 85
Bradbury-Wolff, M., 78
Bradshaw, C., 111
brainstorming, 106
Brand, M., 122
Brazelton, B., 3
Brewster, J., 78
Brindley, G., 138, 139
British Dyslexia Association, 195
Brown, H. D., 51
Bruner, J. S., 14
Burke, J., 88

Cambridge Young Learners Tests,
    145
Cameron, L., 101, 139
candy, 189
capitalization, 88
caregivers, 167. See also parent
    involvement
Carlo, M. S., 123
categories activity, 129–130
Celce-Murcia, M., 52
Centre for Information on
    Language Teaching and Research
    (CiLT), 156, 161
Cervantes, H. T., 192
chants. See songs/finger-plays
character-based languages, 69, 100
Charrington, M., 132
checklists, 109
children's treasures, 7
children's work, assessing, 10,
    155–157
choral response, 53
classroom door displays, 84
classroom management, 187–192
CLT (Communicative Language
    Teaching), 56
cognitive development, 3, 4–5, 7
    and listening, 30
    and vocabulary, 122, 128
    and writing, 99
Collins, K., 83
Communicative Language Teaching
    (CLT), 56
comprehensible input, 13–14
comprehension
    assessment of, 146, 147–148
    and reading, 71, 86–90
    strategies for, 88–90
computers

Internet, 199–200
    and writing, 100
Concentration, 57, 131
configuration, 75
consonant-vowel-consonant (CVC)
    pattern, 80
content area writing, 115–117
context
    and comprehensible input, 13
    and comprehension, 88
    and vocabulary, 124–125
conversations
    and assessment, 160
    and eavesdropping, 24
    and interest/development
        survey, 9–10
Cook, G., 22, 46
Cook, V., 6
coursebook activities
    assessment, 157–162
    listening, 40–42
    reading, 72, 76, 91
    speaking, 55–56, 63–66
    vocabulary, 121, 130, 132–134
    writing, 114–117
Covill, C., 132
Cowley, J., 81–82
cultural differences, 14, 167, 177
cursive writing, 99–100
CVC (consonant-vowel-consonant)
    pattern, 80

Daniels, H., 139
Decarrico, J. S., 124
decoding, 69, 70–71
    and listening, 25
    and phonics-based instruction,
        76, 77
deep processing, 126
development, 2–6
    assessment of, 6–12
developmentally appropriate
    instruction, 2–3
dialogues, 54
Diaz-Rico, L., 69, 70
dictionaries, 126–127, 133–134
direct instruction, 123
Dorn, L. J., 98
drawings
    and assessment, 10
    and listening, 38
    and parent involvement, 171
drills, 52–53
dyslexia, 193–195

eavesdropping, 24
Eccles, J., 167

Index

Echevarria, J., 62
editing, 102, 109
"The Eensy Weensy Spider," 32
Eisele, B., 158
Eisele, C., 158
Elkind, D., 182
Ellis, G., 78
Ellis, R., 62
emergent literacy, 77
emotional/social development, 3, 4, 7, 46–47
engaging learners, 93–94
Engel, B., 155
English as a Foreign Language vs. English as a Second Language, 144
English Language Learner KnowledgeBase, 149
English-language books, obtaining, 83
environmental print
    and comprehensible input, 13
    and reading, 83–84, 91
    and writing, 103–104, 110
error correction
    and reading, 80
    and speaking, 60–62
    and writing, 108–109
Esch, E. H., 183
evaluation, 138, 139
expectations, realistic, 49, 141, 198

feedback, 191. *See also* error correction
feely boxes, 13
Finchler, J., 86–87
fine motor skills, 5, 100
finger-plays. *See* songs/finger-plays
first-language development. *See* native-language development
fishbowl technique, 54–55, 63
Fisher, P., 126
Fitzgerald, P., 54
Flege, J. E., 182
fluency, 56, 61, 101
following instructions, 27, 30
formal assessment, 143–145
Fowles, C., 127
Freeman, D., 12, 139
Freeman, Y., 12, 139

Gall, M., 102
Gamboa, F. C., 159
games, 57, 83
Gardner, Howard, 197
Georgiou-Ioannou, S., 139
"Goldilocks and the Three Bears," 34–35

Gove, 107
Graham, M., 54
grammar, 31, 37
graphic organizers, 88–90
Greenspan, S., 3
Gronlund, G., 155
gross motor skills, 5
group writing, 112
Gunning, T., 28

Hadfield, J., 111
Hanlon, R., 158
Hanlon, S., 158
Harold, R., 167
"Head and Shoulders," 32
hearing, 22–23
hearing impairment, 22–23, 193
Heilman, A. W., 29, 76
high-frequency words, 122
Hill, D., 72
"The Hokey-Pokey," 48, 53
holistic rubrics, 148
homework, 177
Hong, E., 177
Hudelson, S., 83
Hughes, A., 140
Hurley, S. R., 151
Hyltenstam, K., 182

IATEFL (International Association of Teachers of English as a Foreign Language), 200
inconsistent development, 5
indirect instruction, 123
information, reading for, 73–74, 76, 88, 92
innovations, 48–49
instructions
    for assessment, 142, 147
    and listening, 27, 30
interest/development survey, 7–10, 19–20
International Association of Teachers of English as a Foreign Language (IATEFL), 200
Internet, 199–200
inventive spelling, 113

Krashen, S. D., 12, 13
KWL charts, 89

language acquisition, 12–13
    and listening, 22
    and speaking, 46
language experience approach, 85
language learning, 12–13
learning centers
    and comprehensible input, 13

    and reading, 84–85
    and writing, 112
learning channels
    and listening, 25–27, 30, 38
    and multiple intelligences, 197–198
    and vocabulary, 126
Learning Disabilities Association of America, 196
Levick, M., 10
Levinson, M., 167
Lewis, G., 199
lexical fields, 121
Lightfoot, S-L., 167
Linse, C., 31, 102
listening, 22–44
    assessment of, 146–148, 157–158
    and hearing impairment, 22–23
    and learning channels, 25–27
    and reading, 25
    as receptive skill, 24–25
    skills for, 27–29
    and sounds, 23–24
    and speaking, 25
    and vocabulary, 31, 33, 122
    See also listening activities
listening activities, 30–42
    coursebook activities, 40–42
    drawing, 38
    minimal pairs, 39
    rhyming words, 38–39
    songs/finger-plays, 32–33
    storytelling, 33–36
    syllable clapping, 38
    TPR overview, 30–32
    yes/no cards, 36–37
listening capacity, 28
listening center, 13
literature-based approach, 78

Marinova-Todd, S., 182
Marshall, D. B., 182
Mazurek, 192
M-bags, 83
McCaleb, S. P., 167
McIntosh, M., 54
McKee, D., 93
McKeown, M. G., 122, 124
mean length of utterances (MLU), 50
Methold, K., 55
Milgram, R., 177
minimal pairs, 39
mirrors, 60

Index

MLU (mean length of utterances), 50
Moats L. C., 70
modeling, 8
  and comprehensible input, 13
  and error correction, 61
  and fishbowl technique, 54–55
  and writing, 110–111
Moon, Jayne, 7
moral development, 3
morphemes, 50
motivation, 6
Mrs. Wishy-Washy (Cowley), 81–82
multiple intelligences, 197–198
multi-sensory input. *See* learning channels
Murphy, J., 39
mystery words activity, 130

names, children's, 83
National Institute of Child Health and Human Development, 123, 126
Nation, I. S. P., 122
native language
  and classroom management, 191–192
  and speaking, 63
  transitioning from, 141–142, 192
  See also native-language development
native-language development
  and parent involvement, 184
  and reading, 69–70, 72
  and speaking, 51–52
  and writing, 98
Nicholson-Nelson, K., 197
noise level, 62
Northwest Regional Education Laboratory, 155
notebooks, 127
Not Now, Bernard (McKee), 93–94
Nunan, D., 56, 182

observation, 7
Olson, C. B., 98
O'Malley, K., 86–87
open-ended letters, 174
Optiz, M., 81
overgeneralization, 51–52

parent involvement, 166–185
  and classroom management, 188
  and extra linguistic exposure, 183
  and home language enrichment, 183–184
  and homework, 177
  importance of, 166–167
  indirect, 168
  and language barriers, 169–170, 177
  learning about children's families, 170–173
  learning from parents, 173–174
  open-ended letters, 174
  parents as customers, 168
  parent-teacher associations/organizations, 168
  and parent-teacher conferences, 179–182
  and program information, 176
  and report cards, 177–179
  and tutoring, 198
  and weary children, 182–183
  weekend reports, 174–176
parent-teacher associations/organizations (PTAs/PTOs), 168
parent-teacher conferences, 179–182
parts of speech, 121
pattern books (predictable stories), 81–82
Paul, 189
Paul, D., 29
Pavlou, P., 139
pen-pal letters, 102
Peregoy, S. F., 69, 70, 77, 85
personalization, 128, 175
phonemic awareness, 29, 146
phonics-based instruction, 76–78, 79–81
phonological awareness, 29
  assessment of, 146
  and listening, 38
physical development, 3, 5, 7, 100
picture cards, 65–66
picture dictionaries, 133–134
pictures, 13, 31
Piper, T., 28
planning, 189–190
play, 46, 47, 56, 57
pleasure, reading for, 72–73, 76
Popp, M. S., 78
portfolio assessment, 10, 155–157, 161–162
predictable stories (pattern books), 81–82
prepositions, 30, 31
pre-teaching, 123–124
prewriting, 102, 105–107

print conventions, 88
printing, 99–100
print-rich environment. *See* environmental print
process writing, 101–102, 105–110
Procter, S., 54
productive skills, 24, 157. *See also* speaking; writing
professional support, 200
program information, 176
prompts, 171, 172
pronunciation
  activities for, 59–60
  common difficulties, 49, 50–51, 59–60
  and phonics, 76, 77
props, 13, 31
PTAs/PTOs (parent-teacher associations/organizations), 168
publishing, 101, 102, 109–110
punctuation, 88
puppets, 33, 54

questioning techniques, 86–88

readiness skills, 27
reading, 69–96
  assessment of, 151–153
  and configuration, 75
  elements of, 69–71
  and listening, 25, 28–29
  reasons for, 71–74
  teaching approaches, 75–78
  and vision impairment, 74
  and vocabulary, 77, 122
  See also reading activities
reading activities, 78–94
  comprehension strategies, 88–90
  engaging learners, 93–94
  environmental print, 83–84, 91
  language experience approach, 85
  learning centers, 84–85
  own words, 85–86
  pattern books, 81–82
  phonics, 79–81
  questioning techniques, 86–88
  sight words, 83
  strategy variety, 90–93
reading aloud, 72
realia, 13, 31
realistic expectations, 49, 141, 198
receptive skills, 24–25, 157. *See also* listening; reading
reliability, 140, 145

Index

repetition
and listening, 35
and reading, 81–82
and speaking, 48
and tongue twisters, 60
See also auditory patterns
report cards, 177–179
revising, 102, 107–109
rewards, 189
rhyming words, 38–39
riddles, 142
Riley, P., 183
role-playing, 47, 54
Rosenfeld, A., 182
Ross, G., 14
rubrics, 148–151, 153–155
rules, 187–188

Salvador, R. W., 159
scaffolding, 14–15, 22
scavenger hunt, 130
schemata, 13
self-assessment, 156
semantic maps, 89
separation anxiety, 167
Sequence of Events Story Map, 153
Short, D., 62
sight words, 83
Sileci, S. B., 92
silliness, 107
Slattery, M., 54
sleep, 182
Snow, C., 182
social/emotional development, 3, 4, 7, 46–47
Soffos, C., 98
Sokolik, M., 98
SOLOM (Student Oral Language Observation Matrix), 148–151
songs/finger-plays
and assessment, 140
and listening, 32–33
and speaking, 47–49, 53, 59
sound/symbol correspondence, 70–71
speaking, 46–67
assessment of, 148–151, 159–160
common difficulties, 49–52
and listening, 25
uses of, 46–47
See also speaking activities
speaking activities, 52–66
Audiolingual Method, 52–55
Communicative Language Teaching, 56

coursebook activities, 55–56, 63–66
error correction, 60–62
games, 57
managing, 62–63
and pronunciation, 59–60
songs/finger-plays, 47–49
Talking and Writing Box, 58–59
special needs, 192–197
ADD/ADHD, 195–196
dyslexia, 193–195
and tutoring, 198
spelling, inventive, 113
Story Elements Map, 151–152
story maps, 151–153
storytelling, 33–36
storytelling pieces, 33
strangers, talking to, 143
Student Oral Language Observation Matrix (SOLOM), 148–151
substitution drills, 52–53
support, 14–16
syllable clapping, 38

tactile learners, 25–27. *See also* learning channels
Talking and Writing Box
and assessment, 11
and speaking, 58–59
and writing, 108, 112
Teachers of English to Speakers of Other Languages (TESOL), 200
technology, 100, 199–200
TESOL (Teachers of English to Speakers of Other Languages), 200
Testing Miss Malarkey (Finchler and O'Malley), 86–87
tests. *See* assessment
text types, 102–105
"This is the Way We Wash Our Clothes," 48
Thornbury, S., 126
Tinajero, J. V., 151
Tompkins, G. E., 113
tongue twisters, 60
Total Physical Response (TPR) activities, 30–38
and assessment, 147
drawing, 38
overview, 30–32
songs/finger-plays, 32–33, 48
storytelling, 33–36
vocabulary, 122
yes/no cards, 36–37

TPR. *See* Total Physical Response (TPR) activities
translations, 8, 169
trust, 143
tutoring, 198–199

utterances, 46

Vaca, J. L., 107
Vaca R. T., 107
validity, 140, 145
Venn diagrams, 90
Vihman, M., 22
vision impairment, 74, 193
visual learners, 25–27. *See also* learning channels
vocabulary, 121–136
and context, 124–125
deep processing, 126
and dictionaries, 126–127
direct vs. indirect instruction, 123
elements of, 121
and listening, 31, 33, 122
multiple exposures to, 126
notebooks for, 127
pre-teaching, 123–124
and reading, 77, 122
and speaking, 46, 57
See also vocabulary activities
vocabulary activities, 128–134
basket activity, 131
categories, 129–130
Concentration, 131
coursebook activities, 121, 130, 132–134
mystery words, 130
personalization, 128
scavenger hunt, 130
"what's missing?," 130
word for the day, 129
Vogt, M. E., 62
vowel sounds, 80
Vygotsky, L., 14

wait time, 15, 141
weary children, 182–183
Weed, K., 69, 70
weekend reports, 174–176
"What's missing?" activity, 130
Willis, J., 54
Winsler, A., 14
Winzer, 192
Wise, N., 182
Wood, D. J., 14
word for the day, 129
word processors, 100
Word Walls, 114, 122

Index

writing, 98–119
    assessment of, 153–155
    elements of, 98–99
    and parent involvement,
      172–173
    printing vs. cursive, 99–100
    process approach, 101–102,
      105–110
    text types, 102–105
    and vocabulary, 122
    See also writing activities
writing activities, 110–117
    conferences, 113
    coursebook activities, 114–117
    group writing, 112
    inventive spelling, 113
    models, 110–111
    Talking and Writing Box, 108,
      112
    Word Walls, 114
    writing center, 112
writing center, 112
writing conferences, 113

Yedlin, J., 8
yes/no cards, 36–37

Zone of Proximal Development
  (ZPD), 14

Credits